Tim Flannery is Director of the South Australian Museum. He is the author of a number of award-winning books including *The Future Eaters* and *Throwim Way Leg*, and has edited and introduced Watkin Tench's *1788*, *The Explorers*, *The Birth of Sydney* and Matthew Flinders' *Terra Australis*. Tim Flannery has made contributions of international significance to the fields of palaeontology, mammalogy and conservation.

55 Princes St. Prahran
Sandringham line
3RD Station from Flinders St.

Other books by Tim Flannery

Mammals of New Guinea
Tree Kangaroos: A Curious Natural History with
    R. Martin, P. Schouten and A. Szalay
The Future Eaters
Possums of the World: a Monograph of the Phalangeroidea
    with P. Schouten
Mammals of the South West Pacific and Moluccan Islands
Watkin Tench, 1788 (ed.)
John Nicol, Life and Adventures 1776–1801 (ed.)
Throwim Way Leg: An Adventure
The Explorers (ed.)
The Birth of Sydney (ed.)
*The Eternal Frontier: an Ecological History of North
    America and its Peoples*
*Terra Australis: Matthew Flinders' Great Adventures in
    the Circumnavigation of Australia* (ed.)

THE

LIFE AND ADVENTURES

OF

WILLIAM BUCKLEY,

THIRTY-TWO YEARS A WANDERER

AMONGST THE ABORIGINES OF THE THEN UNEXPLORED COUNTRY
ROUND PORT PHILLIP,

NOW

THE PROVINCE OF VICTORIA.

BY JOHN MORGAN.

AUTHOR OF THE EMIGRANT'S NOTE BOOK AND GUIDE WITH
RECOLLECTIONS OF THE WAR IN CANADA
1812—15.

" I was indeed a lone man."
—*Page* 82.

TASMANIA:

PRINTED AND PUBLISHED BY ARCHIBALD MACDOUGALL,
MELVILLE-STREET HOBART.

1852.

ACKNOWLEDGMENT

Sincere thanks to Dr Betty Meehan, Dr Les Hiatt and Dr Alexandra Szalay for their thoughtful and timely comments on the introduction. Any remaining errors are, of course, the full responsibility of the author.

The Text Publishing Company
171 La Trobe Street
Melbourne Victoria 3000
Australia

The Life and Adventures of William Buckley first published in 1852 by
Archibald MacDougall, Hobart
This edition first published by The Text Publishing Company 2002
Reprinted 2002, 2003

Design by Chong Weng-ho
Map by Tony Fankhauser
Typeset by Midland Typesetters
Printed and bound by Griffin Press

National Library of Australia
Cataloguing-in-Publication data:
Morgan, John, 1792-1866. The life and adventures of William Buckley : thirty-two years a wanderer amongst the Aborigines of the then unexplored country around Port Phillip, now the province of Victoria.

ISBN 1 877008 20 6.

1. Buckley, William, 1780-1856. 2. Explorers - Biography. 3. Aborigines, Australian - Victoria - History. 4. Aborigines, Australian - Social life and customs. I. Flannery, Tim, 1956- . II. Title.

994.502092

CONTENTS

Nullemungob
(Murgheboluc

Yawangcontes
(*Lake Murdeduke*)

Kongiadgillock
(*Lake Corangamite*)

Morr
(Mt Mo

Moodewari ⑤
(*Lake Modewarre*)

Barwon River

Bearrock Swamp
(Gerangamete)

Banor
(Sugarloaf Hill) ▲

Bermongo
(Barramunga) ●

Nooraki
(Mt Defiance) ▲

Mangenoa L
(Painkalac Creek)

Bass Strait

*Southern
Ocean*

INTRODUCTION
BY TIM FLANNERY

At 2 pm on Sunday, 6 July 1835, a giant of a man shambled into the camp left by John Batman at Indented Head near Geelong. Batman had departed for Van Diemen's Land to prepare a full-scale migration to his new settlement in the wild country around Port Phillip Bay, but the figure that entered his camp that day was a reminder that the region's European history had begun long before. An astonished Jim Gumm, who had been left in charge by Batman, measured the stranger, discovering that he was six foot five and seven-eighths inches tall (198 centimetres) in his bare feet. Though clearly a European, and 'well proportioned …with an erect military gait' the visitor spoke not a word of English. Instead, he pointed to a tattoo on his arm, which bore the initials WB alongside crudely executed figures of the sun, moon and a possum-like creature. Then, when he was given a slice from a loaf, the word 'bread' broke suddenly—almost involuntarily—from his lips.

Over the following weeks, as his mother tongue slowly returned to him, fragments of the stranger's history were revealed. His name, he said, was William Buckley, and he had been living with the Aborigines for so long he had lost track of time. At first he claimed to be a shipwrecked sailor, but then admitted that he was a runaway convict and begged for a pardon. What he told of his life in the Victorian bush so amazed those who heard him that he soon became celebrated as 'the wild white man'. He was, according to his contemporary and biographer James Bonwick, one of the most 'wonderful characters' that Australian history has ever produced.

Buckley's sudden appearance astonished many because for the previous thirty-two years he had been presumed dead—'perished miserably in the woods' according to Lieutenant-Governor David Collins. Yet all the while he had been living with the Aboriginal tribes of western Victoria. With them he had travelled hundreds of kilometres into the hinterland (as yet unexplored by Europeans), experienced tribal wars, witnessed mysterious ceremonies, and even claimed to have seen the fabulous bunyip.

So great was public demand for Buckley's story that shortly after his discovery an entrepreneur almost tricked him into becoming a sort of theatrical freak show, until the horrified Buckley realised what the game was. He was hardly more co-operative with newspapermen, some of whom assiduously applied 'the steamy vapour of the punchbowl' in an effort to prise his story from him. It was in vain also that august personages such as George Arthur, lieutenant-governor of Van Diemen's Land, made inquiry. Even Governor Richard Bourke himself, who took time out from naming the village of Melbourne to meet with the local celebrity, received just a couple of monosyllables in reply to his numerous and earnest questions. Over the years it was to become a familiar pattern. It mattered not whom the inquirer was, nor whether the questions were learned or salacious—all came away frustrated. John Pascoe Fawkner, one of Victoria's earliest and most illustrious settlers, was perhaps not alone in thundering, after meeting Buckley, that the man was 'a mindless lump of matter'.

And yet, unknown to everyone it seems, Buckley *had* spoken of his adventures. Shortly after he came into the camp at Indented Head he had confided in the Reverend George Langhorne, a missionary whom he was seconded to work under as interpreter, at the salary of

£50 per year. Langhorne found that obtaining Buckley's story was 'extremely irksome…as I frequently had to frame my queries in the most simple form, [Buckley's] knowledge of his mother tongue being very imperfect at the time'. The account, which was later transcribed onto just four closely typed pages, remained 'buried treasure' for nearly eighty years. When discovered and published in the *Age* in 1911 it would revolutionise our understanding of Buckley and his experiences.

  As a result of his silence and of comments such as Fawkner's, Buckley has come to be thought of as a dull-witted giant. Such a man, however, could never have survived the things that fate threw at William Buckley. He may have been poorly educated, but his narrative reveals him as a resourceful and adaptable fellow of some perception and intellect who managed to learn at least one Aboriginal language near-perfectly. It is hard to be sure why Buckley remained tight-lipped for so long. Perhaps he was just sick and tired of being treated as a freak, or maybe his life as a soldier, then a convict, had taught him the virtue of keeping his mouth shut. In a frontier settlement like early Melbourne the habit would have served him well, for rumours about him were rife. John Pascoe Fawkner accused him of conniving with the Aborigines to kill shepherds and steal sheep, while the surveyor John Wedge spread the word that he had been transported for attempting to assassinate the Duke of Kent at Gibraltar!

When *The Life and Adventures of William Buckley* was finally published in 1852, seventeen years after he had wandered in from the wilderness, it was with the patronage of John Morgan, a Tasmanian newspaper editor who had convinced Buckley to collaborate in producing the book. It's difficult to determine just how much influence Morgan had in shaping this remarkable autobiography, but there are reasons to assume that his editorialising was extensive—for Buckley was only semi-literate, and he agreed that Morgan should share the profits from the work.

Life and Adventures appeared just three years before Buckley's death. By then, his story was in effect the only real asset the 'wild white man' possessed, for he had been reduced to subsisting on a government pension of £12 per year, supplemented by whatever he could earn portering, carting and carrying messages around Hobart. John Morgan was likewise impecunious, and it was he who suggested to Buckley the idea of publishing the book as a fund-raising venture.

The extraordinary narrative proved at once contentious. Just four years after its publication the colonial author and historian James Bonwick published his own account titled *William Buckley, The Wild White*

Man and His Port Phillip Black Friends, in which he outlined 'weighty reasons of objection to [the] authenticity' of the account to which Buckley put his name. Bonwick, however, did concede that *Life and Adventures,* is 'an authority for the leading facts of his story'. Indeed there is a tinge of sour grapes to Bonwick's book, for he seems to have coveted Morgan's role. Bonwick had a fascination with early Melbourne and would go on to write the city's history. He shared the streets of Hobart for seven years with Buckley and went so far as to interrogate the man's acquaintances, yet all collaboration with the 'wild white man' was denied him.

Buckley's fascination has proved enduring. More than fifty years after his death Melbourne newspapers were still devoting considerable column inches to his story. Several books and articles have been written about him, and his narrative was revived in 1967, and again (along with related papers) in 1979 and 1996. There is an intriguing novel, *Buckley's Hope* by Craig Robertson, which tells Buckley's story from the imaginative viewpoint and is well worth reading. Buckley is also one of the few Australian historical figures whose name has entered the idiom. 'You've got Buckley's chance, mate' means that you have almost no chance at all; though it seems that the establishment of Buckley & Nunn's department store in Melbourne gave the saying new life as a pun.

Buckley's survival against the odds, both among his own countrymen and the Aborigines, does seem astounding. Because of his height he fought as 'pivot man' in the King's Own Regiment of Foot against Napoleon in the Netherlands, where he was held in high esteem and was wounded in action. His military career was blighted, however, when, on 2 August 1802, he was convicted at Sussex Assizes of knowingly having received a bolt of stolen cloth. He was sentenced to transportation for fourteen years, and in April 1803 was shipped aboard the *Calcutta* which, along with the supply ship *Ocean*, comprised Victoria's 'first fleet'. The vessels were bound for Port Phillip Bay, discovered just the year before by Lieutenant Murray of the *Lady Nelson*. The 300 convicts were under the command of Lieutenant-Colonel David Collins of the Royal Marines, a veteran in the field of convict transportation, having served as Judge Advocate with the First Fleet.

When the vessels arrived in the south-east corner of the bay in early October, many of the passengers were at first delighted. 'Nothing could be more pleasing to the eye than the beautiful green plains with lofty trees which surrounded us. In short the country appeared

more like pleasure grounds than a wild savage continent,' wrote Nicholas Pateshall, a lieutenant on the
Calcutta. The location chosen for the settlement was
Sullivan Bay near present-day Sorrento, some ninety
kilometres south of where Melbourne would be
founded. Despite its beauty the choice proved to be a
disaster, for the soil was barren and sandy, and the
water brackish and hard to procure. Within a couple of
months, Collins and most of the convicts were preparing to desert the place, and it was at this critical
moment that William Buckley made his life-changing
decision to escape.

Buckley was not the first convict to attempt to
abscond, for twelve others had earlier tried, all of
whom, Pateshall tells us, 'had been taken and severely
punished'. Buckley and his five co-conspirators (of
whom Buckley mentions only two in his narratives)
were much smarter. They chose Christmas Eve 1803,
when the officers were presumably well lubricated with
spirits and dead to the world in their stretchers, to
pilfer critically needed goods—a gun, boots, and items
from the hospital tent. A couple of days later, at 9 pm
on 27 December, they made their break, all succeeding
except Charles Shaw, who was shot and severely
wounded. And this is the last, for thirty-two years, that
the wider world hears of William Buckley. When

David Collins, in no doubt of his fate, proclaimed him dead, it was probably just what Buckley wanted.

Buckley traipsed around virtually the entire circumference of Port Phillip Bay before he found his future home on the Bellarine Peninsula, now made famous by the ABC television drama 'SeaChange'. Few parts of Australia can boast such rich resources. Its sea is bounteous, including exposed ocean beaches, sheltered bayside waters, and a variety of estuaries and lagoons. It is blessed with a mild climate and reliable rainfall, and its soils are among the best Australia has to offer. It is also breathtakingly beautiful, as anyone who has looked from the peninsula over the bay to the You Yang Ranges will know. The white sands, azure shallows and brooding, distant hills set among fertile plains that one still sees today would all have been familiar to William Buckley.

Two of the most glorious places on the peninsula became Buckley's principal haunts. One he described as being 'surrounded by the sea and the Barwin River'. It was the headquarters of the Bengali tribe and is today known as Barwon Heads, one of Victoria's most popular holiday destinations. The other, Buckley's beloved Karaaf (or Kaaraf), is a small estuary located just a few kilometres to the west. It is now the site of the hamlet of Breamlea, on Thompson's (or Bream)

Creek. There, Buckley built a substantial hut with turf-covered logs; and the bream, which were then prolific, along with the roots of the yam daisy, formed his principal food. Indeed it was his skill in trapping bream and feeding his adopted tribe that led to him being given a wife.

You can see why the Karaaf appealed so strongly to Buckley, for Thompson's Creek is teeming with life, its muddy flats riddled with the burrows of worms, crabs and shrimp that feed huge numbers of birds and fish. A sand dune protects the estuary from wind, and the landscape, perched between ocean and placid creek, has a deeply appealing aspect.

While the Karaaf has changed relatively little since Buckley's time, other aspects of the region that Buckley describes are now very different. Elephant seals and sea lions abounded on the coast between Indented Head and Torquay, and eels were present in such numbers that they could feed a tribe for months. Water birds dotted the lakes and rivers in almost unbelievable profusion, and included species such as the brolga and magpie geese that today are found only far to the north. Their vast breeding aggregations on the Western District lakes formed living larders for the tribes for months on end, and the birds returned each year despite the hunting. And the basalt plains also were rich in game, including the now vanished plains turkey, along with kangaroo, wallaby, koala and wombat.

In one way Buckley's story of life in this abundant region is deceptively simple. It tells of his adoption by, and life among, the Aborigines of the Wallarranga (or Wattawarre) tribe of the Wathaurung people. They called him Murrangurk, believing that he was a man who had been killed shortly before and who—in the shape of William Buckley—had returned to earthly life. The belief that whites were Aborigines come back from the dead seems to have been widespread during the early contact period in Australia, so in this Buckley was hardly exceptional. His experience thereafter, however, was unique, for no other European lived among Aborigines in a pre-contact situation for so long, and none gained the status in Aboriginal society that Buckley eventually enjoyed. His narrative therefore reveals Aboriginal life from a perspective of extended privilege. Dealing with Aboriginal society before it was so greatly disturbed by the European invasion, it provides a precious insight into an ancient and vanished world.

Given the light it shines on Aboriginal life, the reader comes to Buckley's text brimming with questions. Was he truthful? How much is his story coloured by the years that intervened before it was committed to paper? And what sort of mind was acting as a lens on this lost world?

As to his truthfulness, we know that Buckley could lie when it suited him. In 1835 he lied about his convict past, but that is understandable given his uncertainty about the kind of reception he would receive in the European camp. He also gives three different (though neighbouring) locations as his place of birth. This may, however, indicate an imperfect memory rather than mendacity. And as we have seen, he could remain silent on things when he wanted to. It seems to me that Buckley is not always entirely candid in his storytelling, instead revealing aspects of his experience to serve some greater aim. You get a sense of this secretive, mysterious man in the portrait that adorns the 1852 publication. As he stares out at us from the frontispiece Buckley looks rather like the Cheshire Cat, his lips betraying the faintest of smiles. Yet his eyes look past us into the distance, ignoring us, but all the while fixed on his own, unseen goal.

Despite these caveats, there is nothing to suggest that Buckley is being deliberately misleading about Aboriginal society in his *Life and Adventures*. It is true that he was not a man like Sir Joseph Banks or Watkin Tench, who revealed the newly discovered Australia through the lens of Enlightenment thinking. Buckley was altogether a more simple soul. While that brings its own limitations to the story, it's well to remember that it's sometimes the simplest source that provides the clearest vision.

William Buckley, 1852 by Ludwig Becker

The reader may be horrified to find in Buckley's narrative the Pallidurgbarrans, a people notorious for their cannibal practices 'not only eating human flesh greedily after a fight, but on all occasions when it was possible'. The women particularly were renowned for 'sacrificing' their children. These barbarous 'people' were, according to Buckley, of light copper colour with tremendous protruding bellies, and they slept like animals, without shelter, in their dank Otway forests. Buckley solemnly informs us that a huge fire was set to suffocate them, and that the last survivors were turned to stone. 'We saw no more of them in my time,' he writes in conclusion. It might also surprise the reader to discover Buckley's sighting of the bunyip in a lake at Waurn Ponds (on what is now the outskirts of Geelong). In an eyewitness account that perhaps helped the creature enter Anglo-Australian folklore as a credible entity, he reported that the beast was 'covered with feathers of a dusky grey colour...about the size of a full grown calf, and some-times larger'.

When reading about the bunyip and Pallidurg-barrans, we need to remember that Buckley was a rural Cheshireman who doubtless believed implicitly in the faeries and hobgoblins of his homeland. Likewise, the Aboriginal people who were educating Buckley about their environment made no clear division between myth and material reality; instead both were interwoven in a seamless view of the world. I think that in his discourse on the Pallidurgbarrans and the bunyip, Buckley is describing life through the experi-ential eyes of his Aboriginal family—and this includes the phenomena at the edge of their social universe. There is not the slightest impression that Buckley is reporting anything but what he sensed was true, yet for the modern reader there is equally little doubt that bunyips and Pallidurgbarrans are mythical beings. This aspect of his narrative is something that makes Buckley special, for in a very deep sense he entered into Aboriginal life and understood it as did no other outsider, revealing it to us in that light. It also means, however, that we must be cautious in our approach to interpreting the text.

The more fundamental problem in coming to terms with Buckley lies in reconciling the two versions of his life, neither of which the barely literate man penned himself. The accounts by George Langhorne and John Morgan were written seventeen years apart, and while similar in general outline they differ vastly in tone. This is because they were recalled under remarkably different circumstances, and were written for very different reasons.

Morgan's 1852 *The Life and Adventures of William Buckley* is by far the more famous of the two accounts, and indeed has come to be thought of as *the* Buckley story. One could hardly expect a book written under the burden of financial penury suffered by both Morgan and Buckley to be entirely candid, and as we shall soon see, *Life and Adventures* has its own distinct bias. Langhorne's 1835 account suffers from a different problem. At the time it was taken down, Buckley's English was rudimentary, and communication with Langhorne was excruciating and uncertain. Perhaps as a result it is brief to the point of frustration, the reader heartily wishing amplification of the many fascinating issues it raises.

The most striking overall difference between the two narratives is the lighter mood of the Langhorne script. In it Buckley reminisces fondly about his time among the Wallarranga. He also makes an extraordinary admission, reporting that he was quite aware of the visits of European sealers to Westernport Bay, but that he kept well away from them. He justifies his action by commenting that:

> during 30 years residence among the natives I had become so reconciled to my singular lot—that although opportunities offered, and I sometimes thought of going to the Europeans I had heard were at Western Port I never could make up my mind to leave the party to whom I had become attached. When therefore I heard of the arrival of Mr Batman and his party it was some time before I would go down as I never supposed I should be comfortable among my own countrymen again.

Nothing could provide a stronger contrast to the tone of *Life and Adventures*. Here we encounter Buckley as an abject Robinson Crusoe, who on several occasions is so miserable with his adopted family that he leaves them to live as a hermit. While there is no doubt that Buckley occasionally suffered in the wilds, particularly before he was adopted by his Aboriginal family, it is hard to avoid the conclusion that the stark emphasis on the bad times in *Life and Adventures* is designed to evoke the sympathy of the reader. If so it succeeded abundantly, for shortly after the book's publication the new Colony of Victoria granted Buckley a pension of £40 per year.

Strangely, in light of its tale of loneliness and peril, *Life and Adventures* occasionally exhibits a wry, self-deprecating sense of humour, such as when Buckley recalls that at age fifteen he 'was apprenticed…to be taught the art and mystery of building houses for other people to live in, it being my fate…to inhabit dwellings of a very different description'. Just how much of this endearing quality is due to Buckley and how much is the work of his editor John Morgan, wishing to make the book more appealing, is unclear. Yet it's a kind of humour that is greatly loved by Aboriginal people, and there are hints of it in other writings relating to Buckley.

Reading *Life and Adventures* one could imagine that Buckley lived as a celibate for much of his time among the Aborigines. He is far more candid about sexual matters in the Langhorne account, perhaps because he is closer to the experiences he is describing and has not yet learned how to cloak them in mid-nineteenth century decorum. He says that 'promiscuous inter-course of the sexes is not uncommon, and in certain festivals is enjoined—at certain times the women are lent to the young men who have not wives'. Langhorne adds that 'Buckley says he did not live with any black woman; but I have doubted from circumstances which came under my notice the truth of this assertion, and also I think it probable he had children'. This suspicion received support almost fifty years later when James Dawson, a Victorian pioneer and champion of Aboriginal people, published an account of Buckley by his Aboriginal wife. Her name was Purranmurnin Tallarwurnin, and in later life she lived on Framling-ham mission station in Victoria's Western District. Her account was obtained by the superintendent of the station sometime prior to 1881.

Purranmurnin Tallarwurnin tells us that she origi-nally belonged to the Buninyong tribe and was around fifteen when she became 'acquainted' with Buckley. She recalled that an Aboriginal man found Buckley's 'giant' tracks, and followed them until he 'discovered a strange-looking being lying down on a small hillock, sunning himself after a bath in the sea'. The man returned with others, but

> when they came near he took little or no
> notice of them, and did not even alter his

position for some time. They were greatly
alarmed. At length one of the party, finding
courage, addressed him as muurnong guurk
(meaning…one who had been killed and come
to life again), and asked his name, 'you Kondak
Baarwon?' Buckley replied by a prolonged
grunt and an inclination of his head, signifying
yes… They made a *wuurn* of leafy branches for
him, and lit a fire in front of it, around which
they all assembled. He was then recognised as
one of the tribe…When ships visited the coast
to get wood or water, Buckley never sought to
make himself known to any of them.

Buckley admitted to having had a daughter by his
'Aboriginal wife', probably this same Purranmurnin
Tallarwurnin, yet there is no mention of her in his
own book nor in Langhorne's narrative. One wonders
whether she and the person identified in *Life and
Adventures* as the daughter of Buckley's brother-in-law
(whom Buckley claims to have adopted) were one and
the same. If so, their parting was tragic. Buckley, perhaps knowing that he was incapable of defending her
from attempted abduction or other violence, gave
her to the man 'to whom in her infancy she had been
promised', though this fellow and his first wife were
very reluctant to take her at such a tender age.

There is much in Buckley's account of Aboriginal life that may shock contemporary Australian sensibilities. We want to know how much of this information is true, either of Aboriginal Australia in general, or the western Victorian situation in particular.

Life and Adventures has much to say about cannibalism, and the scenes are both graphic and disturbing. The practice, Buckley tells us, either allows the consumer to avoid an unspecified catastrophe or express grief for a dead child or other relative. On several occasions he describes the practice of eating flesh from the legs of slain warriors which, according to Buckley, was 'greedily devoured by these savages'. Yet he gives as the reason for this 'greedy devouring', feelings of 'respect for the deceased'.

Langhorne's narrative reveals cannibalism in a different light, giving somewhat different reasons for the practice. Here we find no greedy savages, but people who 'eat small portions of the flesh of their adversaries slain in battle. They appeared to do this not from any particular partiality for human flesh, but from the impression that by eating their enemies they would themselves become more able warriors'. Buckley continues that 'many of them are disgusted with this ceremony and refusing to eat, merely rub their bodies with a small portion of fat as a charm equally efficient'. The

Langhorne narrative confirms, however, the practice of mortuary cannibalism for love, relating that 'they eat also of the flesh of their own children to whom they have been much attached should they die a natural death'.

Cannibalism evokes a knee-jerk of horror in most people. Yet the practice has been widespread throughout history, as archaeological evidence from palaeolithic Europe and accounts of the starving attest. The strength of the cultural taboo against the consumption of human flesh may partly be explained by its high biological potential for spreading parasites and diseases like kuru (found in New Guinea and similar to mad cow disease). Yet situations clearly exist, such as during famine or on islands where protein is scarce, in which the benefits outweigh the potential costs. In such circumstances cannibalism is practised for its food value.

Cannibalism in Aboriginal Australia does not seem to have been of this nature. Instead, the practice was often imbued with deep spiritual and personal significance. It perhaps finds its closest analogy in our society in the Roman Catholic rites of transubstantiation and communion. The faithful who participate in these Catholic rites implicitly believe that they are devouring the body and blood of Jesus Christ. In both Aboriginal and Catholic contexts, the ritual serves to link the living with those inhabiting the world beyond death.

Buckley records fourteen conflicts involving the violent death of a tribe member over the thirty-two years that he lived with the Wallarranga. Nine of the casualties were women, seven children and seven men. Ten enemies (two of whom were children) were killed in revenge. Buckley also documents the massacre of a tribe near Barwon Heads, the remnants of whom joined his group. The average size of an Aboriginal tribe was between twenty and sixty families, so the recorded death rate through violence is high indeed. Buckley cites just two principal causes for the conflict: disputes over women, and 'payback killings' following a death by natural causes. The disputes over women, which were the source of all but two of the incidents he documents, often occurred after a corroboree or other coming together of the tribes. They are somewhat reminiscent of the traditional Irish 'Donnybrooks' that followed the day of the fair and their origins were sometimes complicated and historical. Perceived infringements of marital rights or contractual agreements between 'wife-givers' and 'wife-receivers' were very common starting points for these violent interactions.

Just why these bloody disputes were such a feature of the Aboriginal society that Buckley documents is unclear. Some writers have speculated that Aboriginal people had already come under stress and suffered disruption from European influence, but there is little evidence in Buckley's narratives for this. John Wedge gives us some inkling as to why disputes over women may have been fought so persistently when he writes that 'the wealth of the men may be said to consist in the number of their wives'. As Andrew Todd, who was also at Batman's camp at Indented Head makes clear, that wealth was far from evenly distributed. In his journal he lists the family units of the Aborigines he met. One fortunate man is recorded as having four wives and another as having three. A further three men had two wives each, while eight were monogamous, and seven men had no wife at all. Just one unmarried woman is listed. Interestingly, there are indications in Buckley's journal that female babies were more highly esteemed than males, perhaps because of their value at marriageable age.

In these respects, do Buckley's narratives give us a picture characteristic of all of Aboriginal Australia, or was Victoria's Western District a special case? Certainly the Aboriginal people of the Melbourne region and westwards inhabited one of the largest, richest tracts of country the continent had to offer. The abundance of resources to be found there was exceptional, and this seems to have influenced their lifestyle. Unusually, they seem to have been relatively

sedentary; Batman records women moving camp bur-
dened by seventy pounds (thirty-two kilograms) of
equipment, which could hardly be carried every day or
over long distances. There is also the hint of a more
complex social structure in Victoria than was usual for
Aboriginal people. Dawson's informants speak of
hereditary chiefs who were distinguished by their
feather headdresses, and Pateshall notes that on the
eastern shores of Port Phillip Bay he met a group of
Aborigines whose 'King who was with the centre party,
wore a beautiful turban of feathers, and a very large
cloak, he was a man of two or three and twenty,
remarkably handsome, well made, and of a much fair-
er complexion than the rest'. He also records that such
chiefs were sometimes carried on the shoulders of four
men. If accounts like Pateshall's are reliable (and there
is some debate about this) it is easy to imagine how
such a hierarchy might lead to unequal access to
resources and be a possible root cause of conflict—
particularly when the custom of infant bestowal
already meant that young women were sexually
monopolised by much older men.

In Langhorne's narrative, Buckley gives a charming
vignette of how he spent his evenings.

I have frequently entertained them when sitting around the camp fires with accounts of

the English People, Houses, Ships—great Guns etc. to which accounts they would listen with great attention—and express much astonishment...As I always kept up at night the best fire and had the best Miam Miam in the camp...the children would often prefer to sleep with me and I was a great favourite among them.

From what we can read between the lines in Buckley's narrative, everyday life must have been good for the Wallarranga. Longevity was similar to or exceeded that enjoyed by Europeans at the time, and sickness was a rarity. Even lesser irritants such as fleas, lice and the common cold were unknown until they arrived with the white man. More significantly, food was abundant and varied. Buckley never mentions a time of hunger while he is with his adopted tribe. Instead he hints that food was often in surfeit; his people moving on from a lagoon full of eels because they were 'tired...of the sameness of food'. Despite its abundance, the obligation to share food appears to have been strictly felt. Dawson records that the Western District tribes had a custom called *yuurka baawhaar* which obligated a hunter to give up the best of his catch, not even being able to share it with his brothers, but instead having to be content with the least desirable parts.

It is difficult to determine the size of the Aboriginal population of this most privileged part of Australia, but according to a widely travelled and famous Aboriginal messenger interviewed by Dawson, the people of the Western District 'were like flocks of sheep and beyond counting' in Buckley's time.

Imagine what it would have been like to awake on a crisp autumn morning in an Aboriginal camp beside one of the Western District lakes. This is the time when the eels are at their most abundant, and when hundreds of people gather for the harvest. The frost on the grass would have had people reaching for their warm possum-skin cloaks and wood to stoke the embers, and perhaps there would have been some cooked eel or yam daisy left over from the previous night to breakfast on. Then the people would have walked to the great stone eel-traps, covering many hectares, to empty the night's catch. If the return was meagre perhaps some men would wade into the lake to spear the eels they could feel with their feet, or to angle for them with worms tied to a piece of string. Whatever means were used the hunt would not be long, and within a couple of hours everyone would be heading back to camp carrying great bundles of the slippery creatures.

Camp consisted of a collection of tightly water-proof, dome-shaped *wuurns*, each large enough to sleep a dozen people in comfort. Depending upon the availability of building materials they might be constructed primarily of stone or tree branches. In the centre of each was a fireplace to provide warmth. Cooking was done outside.

The camps were kept immaculately clean, for the inhabitants believed that if an enemy found anything belonging to them, it could be used in sorcery to harm them. A trip to the dunny necessitated use of the *muurong* pole. It was used to 'remove a circular piece of turf, and dig a hole in the ground, which is immediately used and filled in with earth, and the sod so carefully replaced that no disturbance of the surface can be observed'.

One can imagine that the afternoon was given to cooking, eating and sleeping, or perhaps to the repair of nets and spears. Maybe some women would go searching for firewood, or yams or other food to vary the diet, while those involved in ceremony would prepare themselves at a secluded location; for at night, initiations and other social events would take place.

Aboriginal people have a natural sense of drama and use their environment to magnificent dramatic effect. I can imagine the glow of a fire that would provide a backdrop for a corroboree, and around it the dimly visible, seated figures of singers and onlookers. Even today the rising of a full moon is often used to heighten the effect, and in western Victoria the dancers may have waited for its silvery light to appear above the crater of one of the area's many extinct volcanos. Only then would the first strains of the corroboree sound out as the dancers, painted spectacularly in white clay, came stalking onto the fire-lit stage to the accompaniment of the rhythmic beating of possum-skin rugs. The celebrations would continue all night as the tribes renewed their ancient ties, until at last the great moon slid below the horizon and the first faint light of piccaninny dawn heralded the coming of the day. Night after night the celebrations would go on, until the fires died to a low crackle for the last time, and the tribes moved on to their winter quarters.

The cycle of life of the Wallarranga seems to have been subtle. Buckley tells us nothing of birth practices except that mothers gave birth unassisted, but as a man he would have been privy to very limited information on this subject. It is known that in the Western District an expecting mother was confined with two married women to assist her. Her own mother would tend to her and her child's needs, or if she were unavailable a professional helper, known as a *gneein*, would be sent for and paid a possum-skin rug to do the job. Once the child was able to walk it was given a name, which might

change several times during an individual's life.
Buckley's Aboriginal name, Murrangurk, meant
'returned from the dead', while some other Western
District names translate as 'bite meat', 'stutter' and
'wattle bloom'. Initiations appear to have been mild,
involving neither circumcision nor subincision.

Buckley documents several methods of disposal
of the dead, including cremation and exposure on a
platform in a tree, both of which practices were
widespread in Aboriginal Australia. Describing one
tree-burial he says,

> They selected a strong…tree, and in the
> branches about twelve feet up, they placed
> some logs and branches across, and sheets of
> bark; on these they laid the body, with the face
> upwards, inclining towards the setting
> sun…The women sat round the tree…in the
> most bitter lamentations…A fire was…made
> all round…and at that side in particular which
> was nearest to the sun at its setting, so that he
> might have, in the morning, not only the sun's
> rays, but the fire to cheer and warm him. All
> things being completed, one word was
> uttered, 'animadiate', which means, he is gone
> to be made a white man.

While it must have seemed to many Wallarranga that things would go on this way forever, Buckley's narrative reveals presentiments of change on the distant horizon, but strangely he plays the main warning for a joke. 'They have a notion,' he declares,

> that the world is supported by props, which are in the charge of a man who lives at the farthest end of the earth. They were dreadfully alarmed on one occasion…by news …that unless they could send him a supply of tomahawks for cutting some more props with, and some ropes to tie them with, the earth would go by the run, and all hands would be smothered…All…were forwarded…to the old gentleman on the other side and, as was supposed, in time to prevent the capsize, for it never happened.

While superficially reminiscent of the story of Chicken Little, I wonder whether this warning that the Aboriginal world was about to change had been generated by events at Sydney Harbour, which for the Wallarranga was doubtless at the ends of their known earth. The catastrophes unfolding there, including the smallpox epidemic of 1789 and the appropriation of land, had repercussions throughout south-eastern

Australia. News of them would eventually have spread though perhaps not surprisingly, given language differences, in a somewhat garbled form.

Given the huge potential of Buckley's narratives to inform us of the amazing world of Victoria's Aborigines, it is astonishing how frequently the work has been ignored, or mentioned only in passing by historians. Where not overlooked, it has often been greeted with scepticism, perhaps traceable to Bonwick's early dismissal of the book. Yet it is hard to escape the feeling that a more important reason may be that Buckley's account of Aboriginal life is so at odds with contemporary preconceptions. Yet another factor may be that studies of Aboriginal Victoria have long relied heavily on archaeological evidence. Perhaps researchers have not known what to do with Buckley's intensely human and confronting story.

Despite its cool reception by some, *Life and Adventures* has been received creditably by experts over the years. Edward Curr, author of *The Australian Race* (1886), was one who knew traditional Aboriginal societies well. 'I think I am right to say,' he wrote, that 'Morgan's *Life and Adventures of William Buckley* gives a truer account of Aboriginal life than any work I have read.' More recently Marjorie Tipping, who wrote Buckley's entry in the *Australian Dictionary of*

Biography, noted that *Life and Adventures* is 'close to fact' while anthropologist L. R. Hiatt has said (in personal communication), 'There is a much higher degree of consistency with modern understandings of Aboriginal social life…than inconsistency.'

Buckley's life after he took that momentous decision to enter Batman's camp at Indented Head reveals much about frontier Victoria. He claims that he played an important role in keeping the peace between black and white, and even that he saved the infant settlement from massacre. There is no reason to doubt him in this, for he had already been playing the role of peacekeeper for some time in the Aboriginal community. He recalled:

> I had seen a race of children grow up into women and men, and many of the old people die away, and by my harmless and peaceable manner amongst them, had acquired great influence in settling their disputes. Numbers of murderous fights I had prevented by my interference, which was received by them as well meant; so much so, that they would often allow me to go amongst them previous to a battle, and take away their spears, and waddies, and boomerangs.

By virtue of his age and peaceful ways, Buckley had become a *ngurungaeta*—a person of considerable respect among his people—and his voice was influential in deciding matters of war and peace.

George Langhorne, who knew Buckley better than anyone else in those pioneering days, wrote that he appeared to be 'always discontented and dissatisfied, and I believe that it would have been a great relief to him had the settlement been abandoned, and he left alone with his sable friends'. Indeed Buckley confessed to one settler that 'he wished the whites had never come'. The stresses of living between the worlds of black and white must, at that time, have been almost unbearable. Usually, of course, only Aboriginal people knew those stresses, but Buckley clearly foresaw the fate awaiting his Aboriginal family and all those he had lived among for so long—yet there was little he could do about it. He records his satisfaction in seeing that justice was done in cases that came to his notice, such as that of a young Aboriginal boy who was wrongly accused of murder.

Yet a much larger episode of murder and dispossession was unfolding, and as a friend of the Aborigines—and one who could report on the evils done to them—he represented a huge threat to many settlers. Neil Black of Geelong probably expressed the prevailing view when he wrote around 1840: 'a few days since I found a grave into which about 20 [Aborigines] must have been thrown…A settler taking up a new country is obliged to act towards them in this manner or abandon it.' Despite these barbaric attitudes, government sensitivity to frontier brutality was growing, and in 1838 the massacre of twenty-eight Aborigines at Myall Creek in New South Wales resulted in the hanging of seven Europeans. In such a climate the last thing Victoria's pioneer settlers wanted was someone like Buckley on the scene.

When Joseph Tice Gellibrand and George Hesse disappeared without trace on a reconnaissance from Point Henry near Geelong in February 1837, many settlers suspected foul play by the Aborigines, and some led armed search parties that committed atrocities upon innocent Aboriginal people. Buckley, who was genuinely fond of Gellibrand, offered to search alone for the lost men. He was probably their best hope of rescue, but in the prevailing climate of fear and revenge his services were not wanted. An unknown assailant maimed Buckley's horse to prevent him from leaving, and afterwards he found that 'some persons were always throwing difficulties in the way' of his work. Buckley soon realised that his position had become untenable. His decision to leave Victoria may have been met with official relief, for he wrote that his work was 'badly appreciated by the principal authorities'.

You get the feeling that Buckley was hated by many in this frontier land, and that had he persisted in championing justice for the Aborigines his own life would have been in danger. It must have struck the 'wild white man' as ironic that he found himself in such a position upon returning to supposed civilisation.

In 1837 Buckley left Victoria for Hobart Town, never to return. There he was appointed by Sir John Franklin, lieutenant-governor of Van Diemen's Land, as assistant to the storekeeper at the Immigrants' Home, a position he held for twelve years. In 1840 he married Julia Eagers who, said contemporary George Russell,

> was as remarkable for her short stature as he was the opposite. When they walked out together, she could not reach his arm; but Buckley got over the difficulty by tying two corners of a handkerchief together. The handkerchief was fastened to Buckley's arm, and his wife put hers through the lower end of the loop.

Purranmurnin Tallarwurnin, Buckley's Aboriginal wife, evidently heard about this second marriage by letter, and when she and the surviving Wallarranga received the news they 'lost all hope of his return to them, and grieved accordingly'.

James Bonwick described Buckley in later life 'aimlessly walking in the streets of Hobart, with eyes fixed on some distant object'. The man was unique among his peers as someone who had not only lived extensively but could communicate on both sides of the frontier. Perhaps the 'distant object' that held his attention was the panorama of the Bellarine Peninsula and the simple pleasures that he experienced to the full there in earlier days. Buckley died on 2 February 1856, from injuries sustained after being thrown out of a gig.

Now it is time to take up with William Buckley in his travels and adventures. It's as well to keep your eyes open and your wits about you as you do.

REFERENCES AND FURTHER READING

Bonwick, J. (1856). *William Buckley, the Wild White Man, and his Port Phillip Black Friends*. George Nichols, Melbourne.

Brown, Philip Lawrence (ed.) (1935) *Narrative of George Russell*. Oxford University Press. (Cited by Sayers in a footnote to the 1967 edition of Morgan.)

Butler, S. (2001) *The Dinkum Dictionary*. Text Publishing, Melbourne.

Curr, Edward (1886). *The Australian Race*. Government Printer, Melbourne.

Dawson, J. (1881). *Australian Aborigines. The Languages and Customs of Several Tribes of Aborigines in the Western District of Victoria, Australia*. George Robertson, Melbourne. (Facsimile: Australian Institute of Aboriginal Studies, Canberra, 1981.)

Hiatt, L. R. (1996). *Arguments about Aborigines: Australia and the Evolution of Social Anthropology*. Cambridge University Press, Cambridge.

Langhorne, G. (c. 1836). Reminiscences of James Buckley who lived for Thirty Years among the Wallawarro or Watourong Tribes at Geelong Port Phillip communicated by him to George Langhorne, manuscripts collection of the State Library of Victoria.

Morgan, J. (1852). *The Life and Adventures of William Buckley* (ed. C. E. Sayers). Heinemann, Melbourne, 1967.

Pickering, M. (1999). 'Consuming Doubts: What Some People Ate? Or What Some People Swallowed?' in L. R. Goldman (ed.) *The Anthropology of Cannibalism*. Bergin and Garvey, London.

Presland, G. (1985). *Aboriginal Melbourne. The Lost Land of the Kulin People*. McPhee Gribble Publishers, Ringwood.

Robertson, Craig (1980). *Buckley's Hope*. Scribe, Melbourne. (Reissued 1997.)

Tipping, M. (ed) (1980). Nicholas Pateshall. *A Short Account of a Voyage Round the Globe in* HMS Calcutta *1803-4*. Queensberry Hill Press, Carlton.

—— (1966). Buckley, William. In *The Australian Dictionary of Biography, 1788-1850* (ed. Douglas Pike). Melbourne University Press, Carlton.

Todd, A. (1989). *The Todd Journal. Andrew alias William Todd, John Batman's Recorder and his Indented Head Journal 1835*. Geelong Historical Society.

Wedge, J. H. (1876). 'Narrative of William Buckley'. Published in: Labilliere, F. P. *Early History of the Colony of Victoria*, 1878: Vol 2. Reprinted in Morgan, J. *The Life and Adventures of William Buckley*. Australian National University Press, Canberra, 1979.

THE

LIFE AND ADVENTURES

OF

WILLIAM BUCKLEY

PREFACE TO THE 1852 EDITION
BY JOHN MORGAN

Editors of Newspapers seldom succeed as authors of works on reality, or of fiction; and the latter are also generally unsuccessful as conductors of public journals. Without making a claim to excellence either in one position or the other, I may, perhaps, be permitted to state my belief that these opinions are at least probable, and my reasons for arriving at that conclusion.

The editor of a public journal—unless it be one of great consideration—goes to the performance of his every-day duty with a full knowledge, that what he has to say, will—if read—be cast aside; not more than one number out of every hundred being favoured with a second thought, or honoured with even a brief pre-servation. However able he may be to give useful expression to his thoughts and feelings, the effects of the ability he displays are but slightly impressive, and, at the best, only transitory. He therefore thinks seriously for a time—forms opinions upon his thinking—and then goes to work, running his ideas—as the sailors would say—'right off the reel': his great object being to express himself sufficiently correctly, and intelligibly, so that '*all* who run may read'; and that HE, running a race against time, may have no part of his establishment for a moment at a stand still. The very close, careful, point-ing of sentences—or portions of them—he does not, and cannot attend to, as the least delay may occasion confusion. He cares very little about it in fact, because he has—or ought to have—sense enough to know, that in a very few hours—comparatively speaking—all his labours will be scattered to the winds, as old gossip, old stories, or old information.

This may be wrong; I do not say the contrary, but merely offer an opinion; and that the book writer goes to his work very differently, because he may be permitted to hope the labours of his mind will live a few years, even if it be only in a first edition. With this feeling, so gratifying to the author, he will be careful as to what he puts before the world, knowing how many there are in it who cannot praise, but, on the contrary, delight to censure.

I allude to these matters, because it may be said by some of the readers of this narrative, that many of the sentences are crude, and unnecessarily short: that they might have been made more interesting by adopting a different style of relation. I beg those who may think this, to understand, that the Hero of these adventures can *neither read nor write*, and, that consequently, I have had the laborious task of connecting circumstances together (so as to make them intelligible) from rough notes and memoranda, made at various times, and by conversations, noting the points down in the shape of questions and answers, as I went on.

I trust this fact will be fairly considered by the critic, who may feel disposed—at his pleasure—to find fault with *the style* of this history, written and published, as it has been, under circumstances of peculiar difficulty. As to *the matter* of which it is composed, I have only to say, that I believe it to be faithful: not only because he who is the subject of it, has assured me of its truthfulness, but from my own personal acquaintance for several years with the habits of the Aboriginal inhabitants of the Australian Continent, and previously with those of other countries, in every quarter of the world.

This circumstance, I believe, first induced him to solicit me to edit a history of his life, but it is several years since that application: both of us having during the interval been otherwise occupied. At length, he having been discharged from government employ, and pensioned off on the *large* salary of twelve pounds per annum; and myself having retired from the very *lucrative* occupation of a colonial newspaper editor, I undertook the task, for our mutual benefit.

Fortunately, we found a generously disposed friend in William Robertson, Esquire, to whom this work is respectfully inscribed in token of our gratitude: that gentleman having kindly undertaken to act as Trustee for both parties, which, as Buckley can neither read nor write, as I have already said, was a safe and desirable arrangement.

It may be proper to explain my reasons for considering such an arrangement desirable. Reader, do not do me an injustice; remember the comparatively humble may follow in the pathway of the exalted, and yet not presume to greatness.

De Foe, the author of the fictitious history of Robinson Crusoe, after the publication of that very popular narrative, and during the remainder of his life, was assailed by the literary assassins of the time in a most unworthy and cowardly manner. They charged him with having surreptitiously obtained the journal of Alexander Selkirk, the shipwrecked mariner of Juan Fernandez. They said that having done so, and given his celebrated work to the world, he derived great annual profits from it, whilst he left poor Selkirk to pine in abject penury. Now although *we* certainly do not expect any such liberal share of fame and fortune by the publication of this truthful history, *I* am most anxious to avoid even the possibility of such a reproach, and hence arises the Trusteeship which Mr. William Robertson has so kindly undertaken.

For a long time a difficulty existed as to the risk of printing a narrative of the kind at so late a period, but at length, Mr. Macdougall, (late of Adelaide,) engaged on convenient terms, to bring the work out; which he has done in a manner creditable to himself, and to the colony.

I regret to say, the admirable likeness of William Buckley is the only illustration I can give, the great anxiety for gathering the golden harvest in Victoria, having driven not only the artizan, but the artist, from off the course of his usual industry.

I have nothing more to add by way of preface, or introduction: as for apologies for unavoidable imperfections, I make none—why should I?

In giving the history of a life in the first person, and under such peculiar circumstances, I have endeavoured to express the thoughts of a humble, unlearned man, in that language of simplicity and truth which, in my mind, is best suited to the subject, and to the circumstances as they passed in review before me.

I have anxiously sought to induce a reliance upon Providence in all cases of danger and difficulty, having myself escaped so often from imminent and immediate peril. That man is the best able to judge of the value of God's Providence who has seen His power evinced in the various ways made manifest in the battlefield, in the boundless forest, on the ocean wave; of which those

'Who live at home at ease,'

know nothing, except by reading, and by the labours of others—the Sailors, the Soldiers, the Explorers—the Pioneers of the world.

To them, to all, I now respectfully submit this book.

John Morgan
Hobart, 22 March 1852.

CHAPTER I

*Poor is the friendless
Master of a world*

Buckley's Birth, Parentage, and Education —
Apprenticed to a Bricklayer — Runs away and Enlists
for a Soldier — Joins the Cheshire Militia,
and then a Regiment of the Line — Embarks for
Holland — Battle between the French and Allied
Forces — Returns to England — Gets in bad
company: tried and sentenced — Goes in the *Calcutta*,
with a party of convicts to Port Phillip — Ship arrives
— Prisoners and the Guard of Marines land —
Absconds, with several others — Separates from his
companions — Alone in the Wilderness —Sufferings
in the Bush — Nooraki.

I was born in the year 1780, at Macclesfield, in the County of Cheshire, England. My parents were humble people, who honestly provided for the support of themselves, and a family of two girls and two boys, by cultivating a small farm in that neighbourhood. What has become of my brother and sisters, is not known to me; but a short time since I heard the former was still living at Middlewitch, also a town in Cheshire, and celebrated for its salt works.

The wandering, extraordinary life I have led, has naturally obliterated from my memory, many of the earlier scenes of my childhood; but few presenting themselves before me occasionally at this period, and those only as a dream. The following are however still vivid to my mind.

I remember, that from some circumstance or other, I was adopted by my mother's father, and that I was sent by him to an evening school, where I was taught to read; and that when about fifteen years of age, I was apprenticed by the same good old man to a Mr. Robert Wyatt, a Bricklayer, residing in that neighbourhood, to be taught the art and mystery of building houses for other people to live in—it being my fate, as will presently be seen, during thirty-two years, to inhabit dwellings of a very different description, having for their roofs only the wide spread of Heaven. Having been removed in the first instance from the immediate charge of my parents, I was, I suppose, not so strictly treated by the old people as I should have been, as a boy, and hence the restraints imposed upon me by my master, and his very proper endeavours to make me useful and industrious were considered hardships and punishments, unnecessarily and improperly inflicted. This feeling, in time, completely unsettled me, and my uncontrolled discontent mastering my boyish reason, when I was about nineteen, I determined to enlist as a soldier, and to win glorious laurels in the battle-field, taking my chances of becoming either a corporal, or a colonel,—I cared not which; neither did I very well understand the difference between the two positions, or the career of dangers, trials, and sufferings, upon which I was entering.

Acting upon these impulses, I enlisted in the Cheshire Militia, receiving ten guineas as a bounty, which sum I thought would prove inexhaustible; but, at the end of about a year, I took another bounty, having volunteered into the Fourth, or King's Own Regiment of Foot, then laying at Horsham Barracks. The Regiment was commanded by a Lieutenant-Colonel Dixon, a very excellent officer, and in about six weeks after joining, we were ordered to embark for Holland, where His Royal Highness the Duke of York, at the head of the British army, was endeavouring to sustain himself against the French Republican forces. My Regiment was in the division commanded by the late Lieutenant-General the Earl of Chatham.

It is not the purpose of this narrative, to refer particularly to that period of my life, neither shall I attempt to give the details of the campaigns in Holland: suffice it to say, that in a battle fought in that country, our regiment suffered heavily, and that I was wounded, rather severely, in the right hand. Almost immediately after this action, the Fourth, with other corps, embarked for England, and were landed at Chatham, where we lay some time. Here I received another bounty for extended service, having now been about four years a soldier, and by attention to my duty, and general steadiness of conduct, having acquired the good opinion of my officers. Perhaps my unusual height, six feet five, may also have predisposed them in my favour. It would have been well had I continued in the same line of rectitude, but my imperfect education, and early feelings of discontent returning upon me, I unfortunately became associated with several men of bad character in the Regiment, who gradually acquired an influence over my conduct, which very soon led me into scenes of irregularity, and riotous dissipation. At length, after a six weeks' furlough, during which I visited my

friends in Cheshire, I was apprehended, as being impli-
cated with those men in an offence which rendered me
liable to punishment. The consequence was, that I was
tried at Chatham, and found guilty, but as the laws were
strangely administered in those days, where soldiers and
sailors were concerned, I do not know to this hour the
precise character, or extent of my sentence.

This may appear strange, but the reader will remember, that transportation, as a punishment on any regular
or fixed system, had then scarcely been thought of, and,
that soldiers and sailors were dealt with more at the
pleasure of the Chief Military, and Naval Authorities,
than by Judges or Justices, many of whom, considered
the army and navy outside the pale of their protection.
With this sentence, whatever it was, ceased my connection with my family, and I have never since heard of
either, or any of them, excepting as I have already said,
that my brother was supposed, a short time since, to be
still living at Middlewitch.

My fortune had now changed. I was a prisoner,
working at the new fortifications being thrown up
for the defence of Woolwich. In about six months,
however, a new light broke out over my unhappy existence, and an opportunity was afforded me of ultimately
retrieving my character, and acquiring freedom: this was
by the determination of the British Government to

found a penal settlement at Port Phillip, on the south-eastern coast of New Holland; that part known as New South Wales being the only portion of the Continent then occupied. Being a mechanic, I, with others, was selected and placed on board His Majesty's ship *Calcutta*, Captain Woodriff. Lieutenant-Colonel Collins, of the Royal Marines, was appointed Governor, and he accompanied the expedition, having with him in the same ship, several officers and a detachment of his corps, as a guard over the prisoners during the voyage, and after their landing. The treatment I received on the passage was very good, and, as I endeavoured to make myself useful on board, I was permitted to be the greater part of my time on deck, assisting the crew in working the ship. In justice to the officers placed over us, I must say, the treatment all the prisoners received at their hands, was as far from suffering, as could be expected, at a time when prison discipline was generally carried out by coercion, and the lash and the rope were, in too many instances, considered too good for *all* who had been convicted. To amend and reclaim, to bring back to society, and to administer hope and consolation, were, in those days, considered the encouragement of mutiny, and hence, to be permitted to live without additional sentences, and summary punishments, was looked upon—as mercy.

At length our voyage was at an end, and the *Calcutta* came to an anchor within the Heads, at about two miles from what is now known as Point Lonsdale.

The Natives call that place Koonan, which means eels, that fish being in great abundance in almost all the streams running into Port Phillip. The particular locality had been chosen as the site of a penal station, it being six hundred miles from the nearest settlement, Sydney, and the chances of escape offered to the prisoner being, therefore, very few. In a short time the Marines and convicts landed, and encamped. A distinction was made between the mechanics and the rest of the prisoner people, the former being permitted to hut themselves outside the line of sentinels, whilst the labourers were placed under a more careful control. This was necessary, as the lime-burners, brickmakers, and sawyers, were compelled to work in all directions, and at a distance from the encampment. A magazine and a store-house were the first public buildings commenced, and at the former I had been employed about three months, when I determined on endeavouring to make my escape, and to get, if possible, to Sydney. The attempt was little short of madness, for there was before me the chances of being retaken, and probable death, or other dreadful punishment; or again, starvation in an unknown country inhabited by savages, with whose language and habits,

I was totally unacquainted, besides the dangers innumerable which the reader may in part imagine, but which no man can describe—no, not even myself; although, by the merciful providence of God, I surmounted them all.

These perils and difficulties are now passed; they were then staring me in the face; but possessed of great personal strength, a good constitution, and having known what might be done by courageous men when combating for life and liberty, I determined on braving everything, and, if possible, making my escape. Perhaps my unsettled nature in a great measure induced this, and, that my impatience of every kind of restraint, also led to the resolution. However this may be, four of us agreed to take to the bush, as absconding is called, and being allowed the use of a gun for killing kangaroo and opossums, we made up our minds to start the first dark night, taking it with us, and as much provisions as we could muster.

The opportunity soon offered and we left, as we hoped, unobserved; we however were not so fortunate, for one of the sentinels challenged, and receiving no answer, immediately fired, shooting the last man of the four of us, as I thought, dead; at least, I never after saw, nor heard of him. After running the greater part of the first three or four hours, to make our escape the more certain, we halted for rest and refreshment. We were now fairly launched on our perilous voyage, and it became necessary to reflect on our position, and to examine our resources. The latter consisted of sundry tin pots, an iron kettle, the fowling-piece already mentioned, and a few days' rations. We now pushed on again until we came to a river, and near the bay; this stream the natives call Darkee Barwin: here we rested until daylight, and then prepared to renew our march. Early in the morning, a large party, or tribe of the natives, was seen, armed with spears; and, thinking to alarm them by so unusual a sound, I fired the piece, on hearing which, they retired hurriedly into the bush. I should here observe, that we had now very little apprehension of being retaken, believing the opinion of Governor Collins to be, that any prisoner attempting to escape, would gladly deliver himself up, rather than perish of hunger; besides, we had, by the rapid rate at which we had travelled during the night, placed a considerable distance between us and the encampment. Light marching order being very desirable, when starting on our first day's march, we resolved on parting company with the iron kettle, as a useless article, and therefore threw it into the scrub, where it was found thirty-two years after by a party of men clearing ground for agricultural purposes.

Our next business was to cross the river, but as all of us could not swim, I passed first to try its depth, and after considerable difficulty succeeded in getting my companions over, and then I swam over again for their clothes, being the best swimmer of the party. That night we reached to about twenty miles distant from what is now the City of Melbourne, and halted there until the morning, when we crossed the Yarra River; and, after passing over extensive plains, reached the Yawang Hills, where we finished the last particle of bread and meat that we had, not having divided our rations properly, and taken the precautions necessary to avoid starvation. Here we remained the night; the next morning, I told my companions that we must make for the beach to look for food, or death was certain. They agreed with this suggestion, and after a long and weary march we again made the shore of the bay, and finding a few shell fish, with them appeased our hunger. At a place the natives call Kooraioo, in an extensive bay, we were so fortunate as to find a well of fresh water, and here we remained the night—the following day continuing our course along the beach gathering shell fish, until we reached a place called Woodela, signifying rock. Here we again rested, if rest it might be called, suffering as we were from the want of the absolute necessaries of life: the fish although preserving it, affecting us all very severely. The next day our route was the same, and as we saw several native huts in our journey, we were hourly expecting to fall in with one of the tribes, hunting or fishing on that part of the coast. Another day's travel brought us to a little island, called Barwal, which we could reach at low water, and here we halted several days to recover our strength, which was by this time greatly exhausted. We found about this place a sort of gum, which, when placed over a fire became soft, and palatable; on this, and fish, we subsisted. From Barwal, we could see the *Calcutta* at anchor on the opposite side of the bay. The perils we had already encountered damped the ardour of my companions, and it was anxiously wished by them that they could rejoin her, so we set about making signals, by lighting fires at night, and hoisting our shirts on trees and poles by day. At length a boat was seen to leave the ship and come in our direction, and although the dread of punishment was naturally great, yet the fear of starvation exceeded it, and they anxiously waited her arrival to deliver themselves up, indulging anticipations of being, after all the sufferings they had undergone, forgiven by the Governor. These expectations of relief were however delusive; when about half way across the bay, the boat returned, and all hope vanished. We remained in the same place, and living in the same way, six more days, signalizing all the time, but without success, so that my companions seeing no probable relief, gave themselves up to despair, and lamented bitterly their helpless situation.

At the end of the next day they determined on retracing their steps round the head of the bay, and if possible, rejoining their companions at the encampment. To all their advice, and entreaties to accompany them, I turned a deaf ear, being determined to endure every kind of suffering rather than again surrender my liberty. After some time we separated, going in different directions. When I had parted from my companions, although I had preferred doing so, I was overwhelmed with the various feelings which oppressed me: it would be vain to attempt describing my sensations. I thought of the friends of my youth, the scenes of my boyhood, and early manhood, of the slavery of my punishment, of the liberty I had panted for, and which although now realized, after a fashion, made the heart sick, even at its enjoyment. I remember, I was here subjected to the most severe mental sufferings for several hours, and then pursued my solitary journey.

How I could have deceived myself into a belief of ever reaching Sydney, and particularly by travelling in that direction, is to me astonishing; and even if I had

Extended Warranty Pay	Factory Warranty Pay	Internal Pay	All labor charges are billed on flat rate hours unless otherwise noted.	Total Customer Pay
	$0.00	$18.35		$0.00

— Barrett, It's Terry. Are you sitting down.
— I'm seated. It's only half a chair but still...

No one meeting of $

Feb = Barcode
Put school b/c
of GRE/Injury

March = more w
No venue orient
from candy.
Liverpool

April = ₤₤ of reign
Easter

May = ₤₤ of Bout
Quit start
proving court

June = Nothing

July = Rebecca

Aug = Consolamann

Sept = Bill physic odenmer
Nov = Nothing
    = Leave for
Paris

Dec = Barek home

found it possible to do so, of course I should, on my arrival there, have been confined as a runaway, and punished accordingly. The whole affair was, in fact, a species of madness.

During my first day's lonely march, I saw, at a distance, about a hundred natives, in and about some huts built of bark, and boughs of trees, and others of the Tribe making toward me. Being greatly alarmed, I took to the river, and swam across it with my clothes on, and in so doing extinguished my fire-stick, so that I was deprived of the means to cook my food. This was a sad loss, not only as respected the way of making what I could obtain to eat, palatable, but of preserving my health, under the great privations to which I was subjected. I was glad however to observe the natives retiring from the bank of the river to their huts, instead of following me as I expected, and, with this consolation, when I had made my way to the beach, I laid myself down to sleep in the thick scrub, covering myself over with leaves, rushes, and broken boughs. It was a miserable night, my clothes being wet, and the weather cold, it being the early part of the spring of the year. At daylight, I endeavoured to ascertain if the natives were moving, as their huts and fires were within sight, and finding them not astir, I left my uncomfortable lodging, and took again to the beach.

As it was low tide, I found a considerable supply of the shell fish before mentioned, which the natives call Kooderoo; it is the same as the English describe as mutton fish. Its shape is something like that of the oyster, but it is tougher, and larger, and consequently not so digestible. The shell is inlaid with what appears to be mother of pearl. These fish I was now obliged to eat raw, and having no fresh water I suffered exceedingly from thirst until the evening, when I reached the river Kaaraf, a stream of considerable width and depth, I there laid myself down for the night. It was one, far worse than the last, for I had taken off my clothes and hung them up in the trees to dry, covering myself with the long grass as my only shelter from the weather. The next day, I forded the Kaaraf, and having left it and taken to the bush, I suffered dreadfully during the day from thirst, having nothing to allay it but the dew from the boughs which I collected with my hands in passing. Even this supply was very uncertain, on account of the strong breezes which prevailed during the nights.

Continuing my course along the beach, I reached the Doorangwar River, where I took up my quarters in my usual manner, having the sky for my canopy, and the earthy scrub for my resting-place. I did so this night with increased anxiety, having seen several deserted native huts in my day's march, by which I concluded they were somewhere in the neighbourhood; on this account I had avoided going into the bush as much as possible, although compelled occasionally to leave the beach, in order to ford the rivers I had met with on my journey.

The following day I came to a stream the natives call Kuarka Dorla, without having seen any living creature excepting birds, and a few wild dogs; the latter fled at my approach, but their dismal howlings, and especially during the night, added to the solitary wretchedness of my situation. Although so very short a time had elapsed since I commenced my gloomy pilgrimage, I began to find the weather, as I thought, warmer—as if I had travelled into another climate. This increased my thirst, and the consequent distress, which I could in no way alleviate, the streams I crossed being, even at low water, all brackish from the flow of the tide water. Added to this, my only food being shell fish, I suffered much, so exceedingly indeed, that almost regardless of life, I lay myself down for the night in a state of total exhaustion. With the morning's light, however, I pursued my journey, but this day I was more unfortunate than the one preceding, for I could not find a single fish, or particle of any other kind of food or water, and in great pain and misery that day ended. The following was one which I anticipated would be my last, for I could scarcely move my limbs along, and the stages I made, were in consequence, very short. At length I came to two rocks nearly close to each other on the beach; weary and tired, foot sore and nearly heart broken, I laid myself down between them. I had not been there long, when the tide came in so rapidly, that I found it necessary to climb some way up one of them, and remain there until it had receded. The descent was a work of difficulty, having now been three days without a particle of food or drop of fresh water: however, I resolved on making another effort to hobble along the beach, and at length came to the Mangowak, another salt water stream which I forded. I found the natives had been burning the bush about this place, so I carefully examined it hoping to find some remains of fire; and, at length to my great joy, discovered a tree still smoking, and by this means again provided myself with a fire-stick. For a time, however, this was useless, as I had no kind of eatables to cook, and was still without fresh water. At length I discovered a high shrub bearing a kind of berry, many of which I knocked down; but not knowing what effect they might have upon me, I ate of them very sparingly.[1] These berries I found very refreshing, and soon after I was so fortunate as to discover a native well near the bank of the stream, and close to the beach, in which there was excellent water—of which I drank abundantly.

The Almighty indeed, appeared that day to favour me—especially, as I thought, in pity to my sufferings, for I found also a great supply of shell fish: so that I had now food, and fire, and water.

I should have mentioned, that when I parted company with my companions, one of them took with him the gun I spoke of, as having been brought with us from the encampment; indeed, I must here state, that if I omit to place any very precise details, in their particular order, I hope to be excused; because, so many years' wanderings must have impaired my recollection—except as to the more prominent and material incidents of my life.

At this spot I remained more than a week, perhaps it may have been two or three, for I seem henceforward to have lost all record of time, except by the return of the seasons, and the rising and setting sun. With such luxurious living, for one in my situation, I soon recovered my strength, and be assured, I did not fail to offer up fervent prayers of thankfulness to the God who had hitherto sustained me, and for his support under the other trials and sufferings, to which I might be subjected. At this place it rained very heavily during a whole day and night; being the first that had fallen since my wanderings commenced, but I found a cavern near the beach, and in it I sheltered myself very comfortably.

At length, being sufficiently recovered, I resolved on resuming my journey, and by keeping along the beach, found abundance of fish, but very little fresh water—the streams being all salt, or brackish.

In two days I came to a large rock, about a mile long, which the natives call Nooraki. It is sheltered by very high overhanging land, so that the sun seldom shines upon it, the tide apparently never receding from it, as the depth of water seemed to be always the same. I may consider this as being my first permanent resting-place; for the sort of food I had had since I left the ship, and particularly latterly, and the irregularity of my supplies, sometimes starving, and at others, eating to repletion, had occasioned sores, and painful eruptions to break out all over my body, so as to make walking very difficult and painful. I resolved therefore on remaining at this place until I was recovered, and particularly as there was a fine stream of fresh water rushing out of a high rock, near which, I had determined to erect a shelter of branches of trees, and sea-weed. It was a work of great labour for a sick man, but I persevered and finally completed my sea-beach home in about three or four days; there I remained several months. In addition to my supply of shell fish, I found also in great abundance a creeping plant, the flavour of which is very much like that of the common water melon—rather insipid, but very refreshing.[2] I also discovered a kind of currant, black and white, so that I fared sumptuously every day, and rapidly recovered my strength, mentally and bodily. I remember a fancy coming over me, that I could have remained at that spot all the rest of my life; but this solitary desire was but temporary, for, as it was never intended that man should live alone, so are implanted in his nature, social feelings, and thoughts instinctively leading to the comforts of home, be it ever so homely, and yearnings for society, be it ever so humble.

1. Possibly beard-heath (*Leucopogon*).
2. Probably pigface (*Mesembryanthemum*).

CHAPTER II

He stood alone,—beneath the deep dark shade
Of the Australian forest, where the trees,
A century old the youngest of them made
Hollow and mournful music in the breeze

Discovered by the Natives — Visit the Tribe
— Alarmed by Sea Elephants — Native
Grave — Found nearly dead by Native
Women, whose husbands make me prisoner
— Fight — Corrobberree — Unexpectedly
find some very extraordinary Relations —
The first Paletôt — Another Battle, in which
men and women are killed — Bodies burnt
— Challenge to fight given and accepted —
Elopements, and their consequences —
Kangaroo hunt.

One day when I was indulging in these meditations, and gazing round from my Robinson Crusoe hut upon the surface of the waters, I thought I heard the sound of human voices; and, on looking up, was somewhat startled at seeing three natives standing on the high land immediately above me. They were armed with spears, and had opossum skins thrown over their shoulders, partially covering their bodies. Standing as they did, on an elevated position, armed too, and being myself totally defenceless, I confess I felt alarmed; so that hoping I had not been seen, I crept into a crevice in a rock near at hand, where I endeavoured to conceal myself. They were however soon upon my track, and shouting what I considered to be a call for me to come out, I resolved to do so; indeed I could not have remained there long on account of the water. With but faint hopes of meeting with good treatment at their hands, I crawled out from my shelter, and surrendered at discretion. They gazed on me with wonder: my size probably attracting their attention. After seizing both my hands, they struck their breasts, and mine also, making at the same time a noise between singing and crying: a sort of whine, which to me sounded very like premeditated mischief. Pointing to my hut, they evinced a desire to examine it—so we entered. My new friends, if friends they were to be, made themselves very much at home, although uninvited. One made up a large fire, another threw off his rug and went into the sea for crayfish, which, on his return, he threw alive into the flame—at the same time looking at me with an expression as much as to intimate that they intended to grill me next, by way of a change of diet. I can afford to smile, and even laugh now at the recollection; but, at the time, I assure the reader, I was by no means satisfied with the prospect before me, or with my visitors. At length my suspense ended, by their taking the fish, fairly dividing them, and handing to me the first and best portion. Having finished our meal, they gave me to understand they wished me to follow them. To this I hesitated, not being satisfied as to their intentions, but after a time consented. On leaving the hut, two of them went before, and having thus only one to contend against, I thought of making my escape, but my armed guard was too vigilant; so that, defenceless as I was, no safe opportunity was afforded. We proceeded in this way until we came to their huts, two small turf cabins—in each of which there was just room enough for two persons to lay at length under their shelter. It was nearly dark, and finding that I was to have my sentry friend beside me, and that the other two were to occupy the second cabin, my hopes revived—that during the night an opportunity for my escape would offer. He however did not sleep a wink, but kept muttering to himself all the night, so that by the morning I was fairly worn out by anxiety and watching. At daylight they gave me to understand they were going farther, and that I must accompany them. I, on the contrary, thought it safer to come to an understanding at once, and with this view, mustering all my resolution, I intimated a refusal, that I would not do so. After a warm discussion by signs, and, to both parties, by sufficiently significant sounds, they apparently consented that I should remain; but, as they wished me not to leave until their return, my old and nearly worn-out stockings were required by them as an assurance offering. This I steadily declined complying with, so that after sundry striking of the breasts, and stamping with the feet, they were content to leave me unmolested. I watched them until I thought the coast was clear, and then began to consider in what direction I should steer, for I had not now the beach as a guide for my movements. Whilst thinking over the matter, one of them returned, bringing with him a rude kind of basket made of rushes. In it was some of the berries I have already mentioned, which he wished to barter for one of my much courted stockings. I however objected, being resolved on letting him know I was positive in that matter, hoping by so doing to give him a favourable opinion of my determination, on questions which might arise between us of greater consequence. Finding his negotiation useless, he left the fruit and followed his companions. When I thought them sufficiently far off, I took to my heels, in the direction, as I thought, for the sea coast, and fortunately I made it without much difficulty. Going musing along, I came to a high rock against which the waves were beating violently, the sea at the time being very tempestuous: it was a very grand but a dreary and melancholy scene. Whilst viewing it with a very aching and downcast heart and spirit, I observed a small rocky island a short distance from the beach, covered with the strangest looking animals I had ever seen. They appeared to be about four, or from four to six feet long, having a head similar to that of a pig, without feet, with tails like those of a fish, a large fin on each side, and a body covered with short glossy hair: I suppose them to be the fur seal, or sea elephant.[1]

Finding night coming on, having no fire to warm me, and with so dreary a prospect of the future—without food of any kind—I began to repent having left the natives and resolved on returning to their huts from whence I had made my escape. I accordingly traced my way back, but on my arrival found they had not returned. After remaining some hours, I decided on going in the direction I supposed them to have taken, but after a weary march, I found I had completely lost myself, and very much distressed, I laid myself down for the night, within the shelter of a large hollow tree, such as are to be found in the Australian forests. Having secured a fire-stick during the day, I made a good fire, it being very cold, and raining heavily.

I remember I had no sleep that night, for my fire attracted the notice of the wild dogs and opossums, whose horrid howls and noises were such as to render sleep impossible. The cries of the latter were like the shrieks of children, appearing to be at times over me, and at others close to my ear.[2] Under these circumstances, I hailed the daylight very thankfully, and then proceeded on my solitary way, endeavouring to get upon the trail of the natives, who, as I supposed, had gone in that direction. In this I was not successful, and having entangled myself in the labyrinths of the forest, in a country entirely unknown to me, I became at length lost, and remained so for three days, without a morsel of food, or a drop of water, excepting small quantities which I occasionally met with in the clay holes. When I laid myself down to rest hoping to sleep, the same unearthly noises appeared to have followed me, and my mind for want of relaxation was failing, as the minds of the strongest men will fail, under such circumstances. I continued to wander about in this way, subsisting upon succulent shrubs and berries, until I came to a large lake, upon which I could see an abundance of ducks, and geese, and swans, and other wild fowl. From that lake I found a very considerable river flowing, as I concluded, toward the sea. I at once resolved to follow its course; and on reaching its entrance, saw the little rocky island already mentioned as having the seal, or sea elephants upon it; and it was a great comfort to me, to find myself once more not far from my old quarters where the three natives had left me. I soon after arrived at the turf cabins, having now acquired some acquaintance with the locality, and although suffering much from hunger, lay myself down and slept soundly. At daylight, I had the satisfaction to find some of the same kind of fruit the native had brought me in the rush basket. On these I made a great feast, and after remaining there that day, returned to my own hut on the beach. Here I must have remained many months—how long I cannot tell—subsisting as before; but at length it appeared likely that my supplies would fail, and I began again to reflect on my deplorable condition. My clothes were all in tatters, my shoes were worn out, my health was much impaired by want and exposure, and my spirits broken—so much so, that I determined on retracing my steps in order to regain the ship in the event of her remaining in the bay, and with the hopes of rejoining my companions, should they be still in existence. The winter was fast approaching, the weather had set in dreadfully cold and tempestuous, so that it was not without great difficulty I could go down amongst the rocks for shell fish, which, as I have already said, were now, from some cause or other, getting very scarce in that locality. I therefore bade goodbye to my lonely habitation and started on my return.

One night, whilst travelling along the beach, I was completely bewildered, having been stopped in my progress by a high perpendicular rock stretching out from the cliffs some distance into the sea. The tide running in fast, my only chance of escape was by climbing the rock. This I did with great difficulty, and just above high water mark I found a large cavern, into which I crept for shelter. Having had no fire for some time I was again living upon such raw shell fish as I could find in each day's journey, and with these was making my wretched meal, when I found I had intruded upon the lodgings of some of the tenants of the deep, who could only reach their rocky quarters when the tide was at the highest. I was completely horrified and knew not what to do, as it was nearly dark, and they were waddling in at the entrance. To rush out, appeared to be nothing less than certain death; but happening to make a noise, it struck terror into them, and tumbling one over the other into the sea, they left me once more master of the cavern. I remained during the rest of the night undisturbed, and the following morning again pursued my weary way.

Being now very weak from the privations I had undergone, I could only make short distances during each day; and, as the nights were very cold, my sufferings were great, so much occasionally as to overpower my remaining strength and resolution. After several days I reached a stream which the natives call Dooangawn, where I made myself a sort of shelter in the scrub, and in the morning saw a mound of earth, with part of a native's spear stuck upright on the top of it, to indicate its being a grave. I took the spear out and used it as a walking-stick to help me on my journey.

The next day I reached the Kaaraf at high water. In attempting to swim across I had nearly lost my life, the stream being too rapid for my enfeebled state, so that I was carried some way down by the force of the current. I however succeeded in reaching the opposite bank, and then crawled on my hands and feet into the bush, where I laid myself down nearly exhausted, and perishing with cold and hunger, not expecting to see the light of another morning. In this state I lamented deeply the imprudence which had placed me in such a pitiable position, and prayed long and earnestly to God, for his merciful assistance and protection. All night the wild dogs howled horribly, as if expressing their impatience for my remains: even before death, I fancied they would attack me.

At daybreak I went again onward, looking for any kind of food by which to appease my hunger, and at length came to a place the natives call Maamart, where there is a lake, or large lagoon, surrounded by thickly growing scrub and timber. Whilst searching for the gum already mentioned, I was seen by two native women, who watched me unperceived. At length I threw myself down at the foot of a large tree to rest. On observing me thus prostrate, and helpless, these women went in search of their husbands with the intelligence that they had seen a very tall white man. Presently they all came upon me unawares, and seizing me by the arms and hands, began beating their breasts, and mine, in the manner the others had done. After a short time, they lifted me up, and they made the same sign, giving me to understand by it, that I was in want of food. The women assisted me to walk, the men shouting hideous noises, and tearing their hair. When we arrived at their huts, they brought a kind of bucket, made of dry bark, into which they put gum and water, converting it by that means into a sort of pulp. This they offered me to eat, and I did so very greedily. They called me Murrang-urk, which I afterwards learnt, was the name of a man formerly belonging to their tribe,[3] who had been buried at the spot where I had found the piece of spear I still carried with me. They have a belief, that when they die, they go to some place or other, and are there made white men, and that they then return to this world again for another existence. They think all the white people previous to death were belonging to their own tribes, thus returned to life in a different colour. In cases where they have killed white men, it has generally been because they imagined them to have been originally enemies, or belonging to tribes with whom they were hostile. In accordance with this belief, they fancied me to be one of their tribe who had been recently killed in a fight, in which his daughters had been speared also. As I have before said, he was buried at the mound I saw and my having the remains of his spear with me, confirmed them in this opinion. To this providential superstition, I was indebted for all the kindnesses afterwards shown me. In a short time they went away, making signs for me to remain; and on returning, they brought with them several large fat grubs, which are found buried in decayed trees, and more particularly about the roots. These grubs they gave me to eat, and by this time, so changed was my palate, that I did so, thinking them delicious.[4]

I remained with them all that night, but in great anxiety, not knowing their intentions. I thought several times of endeavouring to make my escape, but in my weak state it was impossible. The women were all the time making frightful lamentations and wailings—lacerating their faces in a dreadful manner. All this increased my anxiety and horror, which was added to in the morning, when I saw the frightful looking demons they had made themselves. They were covered with blood from the wounds they had inflicted, having cut their faces and legs into ridges, and burnt the edges with fire-sticks. I understood by their signs, and manner, that they wished me to accompany them to the tribe they had left to procure gum, which was in great abundance at the spot where they discovered me. I consented, and after journeying for some miles through the scrub, and over plains, we came to the Barwin, which we crossed, and then could plainly see the black heads of a number of natives amongst the reeds: appearing to me like a large flock of crows. About a hundred men came to meet us, but the women remained digging for roots, which they use as food: their huts being situated near an extensive lagoon. My friendly natives, or rather new acquaintances whom I had accompanied, took me to their homes, which were merely branches of trees thrown across each other, with slips of tea-tree and pieces of bark placed over as an additional shelter. They motioned me to be seated, but I preferred at first keeping a standing position, in order to be the better able to watch their movements: in the mean time, the women behind the huts were all fighting with clubs and sticks. Presently the men, excepting the two with me, rushed toward them, in order to separate the combatants, after which they brought roots which they roasted and offered me. What the fight was about I could not understand, but think it must have originated in the unfair division of the food.

My presence now seemed to attract general attention; all the tribe, men and women, closed up around me, some beating their breasts and heads with their clubs, the women tearing off their own hair by handfulls. I was much alarmed, but they made me to understand these were the customs they followed, and that no harm to me was intended. This was the manner by which they evinced their sorrow when any of them died, or had been a long time absent; and, as they believed me to have been dead, they were lamenting the sufferings I must have undergone when I was killed, and, perhaps, until my reappearance again on this earth.

They eventually dispersed, leaving me in the charge of the two who had found me in my perilous situation. All was then quiet for about three hours, for they had gone, it seemed, to their respective huts to eat their roots; then there was a great noise amongst them, and a trampling backwards and forwards from hut to hut, as if something of importance was going on. I was naturally anxious at this, not knowing how it would all end; at last it came on night, and the boys and girls set to work making a very large fire, probably to roast me—who could tell? At any rate I supposed it not at all improbable, surrounded as I was by such a host of wild uncultivated savages: however that might be, it was impossible to escape, as I was too weak and terrified at the appearance of all around. At last all the women came out naked—having taken off their skin rugs, which they carried in their hands. I was then brought out from the hut by the two men, the women surrounding me. I expected to be thrown immediately into the flames; but the women having seated themselves by the fire, the men joined the assemblage armed with clubs more than two feet long; having painted themselves with pipe-clay, which abounds on the banks of the lake. They had run streaks of it round the eyes, one down each cheek, others along the forehead down to the tip of the nose, other streaks meeting at the chin, others from the middle of the body down each leg; so that altogether, they made a most horrifying appearance, standing round and about the blazing night fire. The women kept their rugs rolled tight up, after which, they stretched them between the knees, each forming a sort of drum. These they beat with their hands, as if keeping time with one of the men who was seated in front of them, singing. Presently the men came up in a kind of close column, they also beating time with their sticks, by knocking them one against the other, making altogether a frightful noise. The man seated in front appeared to be the leader of the orchestra, or master of the band—indeed I may say, master of the ceremonies generally. He marched the whole mob, men and women, boys and girls, backwards and forwards at his pleasure, directing the singing and dancing, with the greatest decision and air of authority. This scene must have lasted at least three hours, when, as a wind-up, they gave three tremendous shouts, at the same time pointing to the sky with their sticks; they each shook me heartily by the hand, again beating their breasts, as a token of friendship. By this time I was greatly relieved in my mind, finding no injury to me was contemplated, and particularly when they all dispersed to their huts, and I was left again with my guardians.

The reader, in these colonies, will be aware that what I had witnessed was nothing more than a great Corrobberree, or rejoicing, at my having come to life again, as they supposed. After eating some roots I lay down by the side of my new friends, and although so recently highly excited, yet I enjoyed a sleep undisturbed by dreams, either of the past, the present, or the future. In reality, nature had been exhausted by hunger, thirst, and continued apprehension. In the morning I rose greatly refreshed, and found the tribe already upon the move, gathering roots and spearing eels, a few only remaining with me in the encampment. I observed, that one man was dispatched on some errand, and as he was leaving, they pointed out to me the way he was going for some particular kind of food, or on a message to another tribe, in which message I was in some way or other interested.

Finding myself now tolerably at home, I evinced a desire to make myself useful, by fetching water, carrying wood, and so forth. I went to the river one day for the purpose of having a bathe, but was not long absent before I was missed and an alarm raised; for they thought I had deserted. Search was made in all directions, and just as I returned the messenger came back who had been sent away, as I supposed, to another tribe, bringing with him a young man; who came, as it appeared, to invite the others to their encampment. The following day therefore, our tribe left the borders of the lagoon, taking me with them, and after a tramp through the bush of a few miles, we arrived and took up our quarters, not with the strangers, but at some distance from them, where we erected our temporary huts, or shelters for the night. I was soon afterwards transferred to the charge of a man and woman of the tribe we had come to visit; the man being brother to the one who had been killed, from whose grave I had taken the spear; the woman was my new guardian's wife, and the young man who had visited us, was their son; and, consequently, according to their order of thinking, my very respectable and interesting nephew. It may be taken as certain, that I looked on him, as a very unaccountable relative, one I little thought of meeting in such a place, or in that manner; at any rate there was one consolation, if he was not very wise after the fashion of more civilized men, he could not display great foolishness in his expenditure; and, that there was, therefore, no great chance of his uncle's having to pay his tailor's, or other bills: a consolation many uncles would be very glad to possess with equal security.

That night there was another great Corrobberree, with shakes of the hand, and congratulation at my return. When these ceremonies were over, I went with my new relations to their hut, where they hospitably regaled me with roots, and gum, and with opossum roasted after their fashion. This was the first animal food I had taken since parting with my companions from the *Calcutta*, and it was to me a most delicious feast. They presented me also with an opossum-skin rug, for which I gave my new sister-in-law my old jacket in exchange, although it was by this time very much the worse for wear. I need scarcely say, this paletôt[5] added much to the elegance of her appearance, or, that these interchanges of attractive civility had great effect in cementing our family acquaintance.

At break of day, I heard a great noise and talking; at length I saw that a quarrel had ensued, for they began to flourish their spears as a token of hostilities. I should here observe, that these spears are very formidable weapons, about twelve feet long, sharp at one end; others are about half that length, being made of a kind of reed with pointed sticks joined to them; these are sharpened with hard cutting stones, or shells. The boomerang is another weapon of war, something like a half-moon. The throwing-stick is one made, or shaped, for flinging the spears.

The colonial reader is aware of all this, but I beg him, or her, to remember, that I cherish the hope of my adventures being read elsewhere, as well as in the Australian Colonies; and that this circumstance will be received as a sufficient apology for the insertion of particulars, which, otherwise, might very properly be considered useless.

After a little time, and a great deal of challenging bluster, the two tribes commenced fighting in reality. When my relations, for so for convenience, I suppose, I must sometimes call them, saw what was going on, they led me a short distance off, where they remained with me, looking at the conflict. It was anything but play work—it was evidently earnest. One man was speared through the thigh, and removed into the bush, where the spear was drawn. A woman of the tribe to which I had become attached, was also speared under the arm, and she died immediately. At last peace was restored, and the parties separated, except about twenty of the tribe to which the woman belonged who had been killed; these made a large fire, threw her body upon it, and then heaped on more wood, so that she was burnt to ashes; this done, they raked the embers of the fire together, and stuck the stick she used to dig roots with upright at the head. After this ceremony they all left, except my supposed relations, in whose care I was, and one other family, with whom we went into another part of the bush, where we remained for a considerable time without anything particular occurring, subsisting almost entirely upon roots which the women sought daily, whilst the men procured opossums occasionally, which they dragged from the hollow and decayed branches of trees. They sometimes speared kangaroo, which they skin with sharp stones and muscle-shells. That was the first time I tasted the flesh of the boomer, and found it very excellent. Relying upon my friendship, they now furnished me with a spear, and a wooden tomahawk. In a few weeks—but as I have already said, I have now no recollection of time—we left this place and joined a friendly tribe, about fifty in number, and on the evening of our meeting had a Corrobberree. The next day we all started together to meet another tribe; but on joining, from some cause or other, they quarrelled, commenced fighting, and two boys were killed. I could not then understand what all these quarrels were about, but afterwards understood that they were occasioned by the women having been taken away from one tribe by another; which was of frequent occurrence. At other times they were caused by the women willingly leaving their husbands, and joining other men, which the natives consider very bad.

When these fights occurred, I was always kept in the rear. After the skirmish just mentioned was over, the tribe to whom the boys belonged retired farther into the bush, when we made our huts, as I have described, with boughs and bark. Suddenly in the night, the others came upon our party and drove us away. The bodies of the two boys who were killed were laying in one of the huts, so they cut off their legs and thighs, carrying them away; the remains of their bodies our people burned in the usual manner; we then left for the sea side. Soon after a messenger was sent to another tribe, with whom they had a quarrel about the women; the message was to say they would meet them at a certain place to fight it out. In about four days he returned, with information that the challenge was accepted; so we went there, I, of course, not then being conscious of what we were going for. On our arrival at the battle ground, about twenty miles distant, we found five different tribes all collected together, and ready for action. The fight commenced immediately, and it lasted about three hours, during which three women were killed—for strange to say, the females in these quarrels generally suffered the most. These continual contests alarmed me, for the contending parties were always pointing toward me, as if I had been their origin; and I again began to think I should be sacrificed as a peace offering. Quiet was at length restored, and the tribe we had joined separated from the others, and came toward where I was standing. Having formed themselves into a sort of guard, they marched me back to the other tribe, who placed themselves in square, on the spot where the fight had been. On our arrival solemn silence was observed—not even a whisper was uttered, but all eyes were directed toward me, and I again felt that some serious event might be expected, in which my safety was involved. I had a few minutes before seen women and boys murdered in their fury, and it was natural for me to feel alarm under such circumstances. After a while, they all began talking together rapidly, shaking their spears, and jumping wildly about, as if they were going mad; this ended, they gave three loud shouts, and returned to their respective huts—so I was relieved from my fears once more. In the morning, I found the other tribe had gone away, and soon after we left for the place my friends chiefly inhabited, and there we lived for a very long time unmolested, and without anything particular occurring. We remained in peace and quietness, until a messenger came from another tribe, saying we were to meet them some miles off. Their method of describing time is by signs on the fingers—one man of each party marking the days by chalking on the arm, and then rubbing one off as each day passes. After travelling two or three days, we arrived at the appointed place, and found there a great number assembled, not one of whom I had seen before; and that evening we had the usual Corrobberree. In the morning we all went on a hunting excursion in perfect good humour, so that I had nothing to apprehend. It was a kangaroo hunt, and, as this was the first I had been at, I looked on with great interest, for I began to consider myself, by compulsion, a native, and to take a part in all their exercises. Considerable dexterity is used by them in catching and killing kangaroo; for they place themselves at particular spots and distances, so as to drive them into corners like flocks of sheep, and then they spear them without difficulty. We killed several very large ones, on which, with roasted roots, we made a great feast. After that, they all pipe-clayed themselves, and had another Corrobberree, and then, as usual, began to throw their spears about. This I thought would end in mischief, and the women appeared to think so too, for they ran into their huts. My guardians, as a precaution, took me with them. Nothing serious, however, occurred that night. In the morning it appeared that the Pootmaroo tribe had taken two women from the Yaawangis in the course of the night; or, that they had gone away willingly with their seducers. The consequence was another fight, but it ended without bloodshed. The affair, however, was not forgotten. After that, the tribes separated, each going to its respective locality.

1. Fur seals or sea-lions.
2. Probably the call of the yellow-bellied glider, a kind of possum which possesses one of the loudest calls of any marsupial.
3. The name literally means 'returned from the dead'.
4. In fact, witchetty grubs are delicious at any time.
5. A loose jacket or outer garment.

CHAPTER III

Outcast and hopeless, here I dwell
A dreary desert where I roam

I now began to understand something of their language: of their customs I had seen quite enough; but what could I do?—how could I escape?

We next joined the Bengali tribe, and went with them to their hunting ground, a place surrounded by the sea and the Barwin River—each tribe having its particular locality, which they considered a sort of inheritance. Here we erected our huts, and killed a great number of kangaroo. By eating this food continually, I soon recovered my usual health and strength; for my friends, in their kindness, always served me with the choicest portion of everything they had; so that I had great occasion to be thankful. That I was sufficiently grateful to the Almighty, who had so wonderfully preserved me through such extraordinary sufferings and dangers, I cannot say; for my early notions of religion had been nearly destroyed by the unsettled life I had led, and the want of proper moral instruction. The excellent precepts instilled into my mind by my good old grandfather and grandmother had been long since neutralized, or smothered in the camp, in riotous company, and in the bad society into which I had been thrown by my imprudence. Nevertheless, in the wilderness, as I have already said, I often prayed earnestly and fervently to the great Creator of the Universe for health, and strength, and forgiveness.

At this time we killed an emu, a sort of ostrich, a bird of very large size, and excellent for its flavour. It cannot rise upon the wing, but runs with amazing swiftness.

After staying on this hunting ground for some months, I know not how long, we started again for a new locality, our supplies of game beginning to fall short in consequence of our continued hunting. Having arrived at a place good for this purpose, as they thought, we pitched, or rather erected our bark tents, having killed two immense large wild dogs on our way. The limbs of these animals they broke, and flinging them on the fire, they kept them there until the hair was singed, they then took out the entrails, and roasted the bodies between heated stones, covering them over with sheets of bark and earth. After this process, which lasted two hours, they were ready for eating, and were considered a dish fit for an Exquisite. They handed me a leg of one, as the best part, but I could not fancy it; and on my smelling it, and turning up my nose, they were much amused, laughing away at a great rate. No doubt, they thought my having died and been made white had strangely altered my taste in such matters. As for themselves, they set to work with great zest, making all the time motions to me to fall to also. At length, I exchanged my portion with a neighbour, who gave me for my dog's leg a fine piece of kangaroo, my friend laughing very much at the idea of having the best of the bargain.

The natives consider the wild dogs, and kangaroo rats,[1] great luxuries. They take the former whilst young, and tame them for hunting. The man who kills the game seldom claims the first portion of it, but of the second animal speared, if it be a kangaroo, he has the head, and tail, and best part of the back and loins. As for myself, they always gave me a share, whether I hunted with them or not.

My not being able to talk with them they did not seem to think at all surprising—my having been made white after death, in their opinion, having made me foolish; however, they took considerable pains to teach me their language, and expressed great delight when I got hold of a sentence, or even a word, so as to pronounce it somewhat correctly; they then would chuckle, and laugh, and give me great praise.

I now became a tolerable efficient sportsman, being able to throw the spear, and handle the tomahawk very adroitly. They also instructed me in every art they knew. They taught me to skin the kangaroo and opossums with muscle-shells, in the same way sheep are dressed with the knife; to stretch and dry them in the sun; to prepare the sinews for sewing them together for rugs; and to trim them with pieces of flint. I became, also, expert at catching eels, by spearing them in the lakes and rivers; but in the latter they generally catch them with lines—the bait being a large earth worm. Having these worms ready, they get a piece of elastic bark, and some long grass, on which they string them; this is tied to a rod, and as the eel, after biting, holds on tenaciously he is thrown or rather jerked upon the bank, in the same way as boys catch the crayfish in England. Some of these eels are very fine, and large. They are generally—and more easily—caught by the natives during the night, and are eaten roasted. They used to take me out on calm evenings to teach me how to spear salmon, bream, etc. Their manner is to get some very dry sticks, cut them into lengths of ten or twelve feet, tie several of these together into a kind of faggot, and then light the thickest end; with this torch blazing in one hand, and a spear in the other, they go into the water, and the fish seeing it, crowd round and are easily killed and taken. This—as the reader is perhaps aware—is the general practice throughout all the world: and I mention the custom merely as one amongst others. They cook their fish by roasting, but they do so somewhat more carefully than their other food; for they put thick layers of green grass on the hot ashes, and lay their fish upon them, covering them with another layer, and then some hot ashes upon the top.

In this way they bake as well—but not so cleanly—as in an oven.

Before we left this place, we were unexpectedly intruded upon by a very numerous tribe, about three hundred. Their appearance, coming across the plain, occasioned great alarm, as they were seen to be the Waarengbadawá, with whom my tribe was at enmity. On their approach, our men retreated into the lake, and smeared their bodies all over with clay, preparatory to a fight. The women ran with their children into the bush, and hid themselves, and being a living dead man, as they supposed, I was told to accompany them. On the hostile tribe coming near, I saw they were all men, no women being amongst them. They were smeared all over with red and white clay, and were by far the most hideous looking savages I had seen. In a very short time the fight began, by a shower of spears from the contending parties. One of our men advanced singly, as a sort of champion; he then began to dance and sing, and beat himself about with his war implements; presently they all sat down, and he seated himself also. For a few minutes all was silent; then our champion stood up, and commenced dancing and singing again. Seven or eight of the savages—for so I must call them—our opponents, then got up also, and threw their spears at him; but, with great dexterity, he warded them off, or broke them every one, so that he did not receive a single wound. They then threw their boomerangs at him, but he warded them off also, with ease. After this, one man advanced as a sort of champion from their party, to within three yards of him, and threw his boomerang, but the other avoided the blow by falling on his hands and knees, and instantly jumping up again he shook himself like a dog coming out of the water. At seeing this, the enemy shouted out in their language 'enough', and the two men went and embraced each other. After this, the same two beat their own heads until the blood ran down in streams over their shoulders.

A general fight now commenced, of which all this had been the prelude, spears and boomerangs flying in all directions. The sight was very terrific, and their yells and shouts of defiance very horrible. At length one of our tribe had a spear sent right through his body, and he fell. On this, our fellows raised a war cry; on hearing which, the women threw off their rugs, and each armed with a short club, flew to the assistance of their husbands and brothers; I being peremptorily ordered to stay where I was: my supposed brother's wife remaining with me. Even with this augmentation, our tribe fought to great disadvantage, the enemy being all men, and much more numerous.

As I have said in the early part of this narrative, I had seen skirmishing and fighting in Holland; and knew something therefore, of what is done when men are knocking one another about with powder and shot, in real earnest, but the scene now before me was much more frightful—both parties looking like so many devils turned loose from Tartarus. Men and women were fighting furiously, and indiscriminately, covered with blood; two of the latter were killed in this affair, which lasted without intermission for two hours; the Waareng-badawás then retreated a short distance, apparently to recover themselves. After this, several messages were sent from one tribe to the other, and long conversations were held—I suppose on the matters in dispute.

Night approaching, we retired to our huts, the women making the most pitiable lamentations over the mangled remains of their deceased friends. Soon after dark the hostile tribe left the neighbourhood; and, on discovering this retreat from the battle ground, ours determined on following them immediately, leaving the women and myself where we were. On approaching the enemy's quarters, they laid themselves down in ambush until all was quiet, and finding most of them asleep, laying about in groups, our party rushed upon them, killing three on the spot, and wounding several others. The enemy fled precipitately, leaving their war implements in the hands of their assailants and their wounded to be beaten to death by boomerangs, three loud shouts closing the victors' triumph.

The bodies of the dead they mutilated in a shocking manner, cutting the arms and legs off, with flints, shells, and tomahawks.

When the women saw them returning, they also raised great shouts, dancing about in savage extacy. The bodies were thrown upon the ground, and beaten about with sticks—in fact, they all seemed to be perfectly mad with excitement; the men cut the flesh off the bones, and stones were heated for baking it; after which, they greased their children with it, all over. The bones were broken to pieces with tomahawks, and given to the dogs, or put on the boughs of trees for the birds of prey hovering over the horrid scene.

Having apparently gratified their feelings of revenge, they fetched the bodies of their own two women who had been killed; these they buried with the customary ceremonies.

They dug two round graves with their sticks, about four feet deep, then coiled up the bodies, tying them in their skin rugs, and laying them in the holes, with some boughs, and filling them up with earth: a ring being made round each place by clearing away, and lighting fires. After raking up the ashes over each, the sticks which they had used for digging roots were put over them, as I have already described the spears of the men are, who are killed.

They have an idea that they will want them when they come to life again, and the fire left they think will do for them to cook their roots with. Of this provision they generally leave a few days' supply, and whenever they pass near these graves they re-light the fires. The bodies are laid on their sides when they bury them, in the same manner as they mostly lie when living.

We remained by the graves the remainder of that day and the next night, and then proceeded to the borders of another large lake, which they call Yawangcontes, in the centre of an extensive plain. There we made our huts with reeds and stones, there being no wood; so bare was it indeed, that we had to go nearly three miles for fuel to cook our food with. We remained there for many months; perhaps for a year or two, for I had lost all recollection of time. I knew nothing about it in fact, except by the return of the seasons. I had almost given up all hope of ceasing my savage life, and as man accustoms himself to the most extraordinary changes of climate and circumstances, so I had become a wild inhabitant of the wilderness, almost in reality. It is very wonderful, but not less strange than true. Almost entirely naked, enduring nearly every kind of privation, sleeping on the ground month after month, year after year, and deprived of all the decencies, and comforts of life, still I lived on, only occasionally suffering from temporary indisposition. I look back now mentally to those times, and think it perfectly miraculous how it could have been.

After this very long stay, we received a message to visit another very large lake, many miles round, which they call Kongiadgillock. On one side it is very rocky, and on the other are extensive plains, lightly timbered. About four miles from the shore is a small island about two miles square; this island may be reached on one side of the lake, the water being only knee deep, a high bank running out from the shore towards it, and forming a sort of isthmus. On this island we found an immense number of swans and other wild birds. We made our huts a short distance from the tribe who had invited us to visit them, and here we had as many swan's eggs as we could consume; and there were many more: they were the first I had eaten, and I thought them, by way of change, a great treat. The first day we passed at our new locality, the other tribe said they would take us home with them and have a Corrobberree, after visiting the island. On arriving there we found it literally covered with eggs, so that we very soon filled all our rush baskets; they were laying about in heaps, there being nothing like nests. Our friends whom we visited, allowed us to fill our baskets first, and then they loaded theirs. This continued for several days, and each night we had a Corrobberree. At length the tribe left us, apparently in great haste, but for what cause I could not make out, but I anticipated mischief from their manner, and thought some dispute had occurred amongst them on one of the days when I did not go with them to the island. Our tribe did not interfere in any way. At length we started further up the lake, and arrived at a part that is very narrow. Here we killed a great many swans, which were served out to each family according to its wants; their method of dressing these birds is by roasting, as before described. The next day the women separated from the men, and painted themselves all over with white clay; and the men did so with red, at the same time ornamenting themselves with emu feathers, which they tied round their waists: they were in every other way quite naked. Some of them acted as Musicians, beating their skin rugs with sticks, which they stretched across their knees, whilst they were squatted on the ground. They then set up a dance, the men remaining as spectators, encouraging them with cheers, and all sorts of noises. This diversion finished, as usual, with a regular fight, beating each other about with their clubs most unmercifully. I afterwards understood this quarrel to be occasioned by a woman having been forcibly carried away by another tribe: one of those with us. She was living with the man who had taken her, and, as the man and woman were then both present, they wanted to chastise her for not returning to the tribe to which she belonged. In the skirmish this woman was felled by a heavy blow; seeing this, the men began to prepare for a fight also; one man threw a boomerang amongst the women, when they all ran away. The native who had stolen the girl, then came forward by himself and told them to take their revenge on him, and began to sing and jump and dance, upon which her father went up to him. They both remained quiet for some time, when the men called out to the father, telling him to let him have her, as the man she had been promised to was not worthy of her. Eventually the girl returned to her father. She appeared to be about fifteen years of age, and certainly was no beauty to fight about.

We next went about forty miles, I should think, to a place they call Kironamaat; there is near to it a lake about ten miles in circumference. It took us several days to accomplish this march, as we hunted all the way; we halted near a well of fresh water, the lake being brackish, and there was a great plain near us. We here made nets with strips of bark, and caught with them great quantities of shrimps. We lived very sumptuously and in peace for many months at this place, and then went to the borders of another lake, called Moodewarri: the water of which was perfectly fresh, abounding in large eels, which we caught in great abundance. In this lake, as well as in most of the others inland, and in the deep water rivers, is a very extraordinary amphibious animal, which the natives call Bunyip, of which I could never see any part, except the back, which appeared to be covered with feathers of a dusky grey colour. It seemed to be about the size of a full grown calf, and sometimes larger; the creatures only appear when the weather is very calm, and the water smooth. I could never learn from any of the natives that they had seen either the head or tail, so that I could not form a correct idea of their size; or what they were like.

Before we left this place a Bihar, or messenger, came to us; he had his arms striped with red clay, to denote the number of days it would take us to reach the tribe he came from; and the proposed visit was, for us to exchange with them, eels for roots. The time stated for this march would be fourteen days, and the place was called Bermongo, on the Barwin River. We carried our fish in kangaroo skins, and reaching the appointed place of rendezvous, we found about eighty men, women and children gathered together. The exchange was made in this way; two men of each party delivered the eels and roots, on long sheets of bark, carrying them on their heads, from one side to the other, and so on, until the bargain was concluded. In the evening there was another great Corrobberree, and the next morning a fight; because one of the women had run away with a man, leaving her husband. It resulted by her being speared very badly. After a short time the tribes separated, making an appointment to meet again for an exchange of food.

From this place we went to Beangala, which is now called Indented Heads, where we remained some months, until the time had arrived when we agreed to return for the exchange of fish for roots. On this occasion, however, we took kangaroo instead, to a place called Liblib, by the side of a large lake of shallow water, surrounded by reeds, and which they call Bangeballa. Whilst I was at this place, there was one of the most severe hail storms I think man ever saw. The stones were so very large as to strip the bark off the trees as they descended.

Their language had now become familiar to me, and I began to learn by degrees, and by frequent intercourse with the various tribes, something about my shipmates, and former companions. It seemed, that one of them, having, after a few days, separated from the others, was found by the natives and kindly relieved by them; but after some time, they—as it was said—had reason to be jealous of him—he having made too free with their women—so they killed him. The others I never heard anything more about until my arrival in Van Diemen's Land.

1. Bettongs and potoroos.

CHAPTER IV

My far off friends whose memories fill
My throbbing bosom, — do they speak
Of him whose heart is with them still,
Though joy has ceased to light his cheek?

The only ceremonies they use preparatory to marriage are, in the first place, to get the parents' consent, <u>the suitor's best claim is being a good fighter, and an expert hunter</u>—so as to be able to protect and provide for a family. They are not at all particular as to the number of wives such men have; consequently some have five or six wives, and others none at all. If a man wishes to have a man's grown up sister for a wife, he must give his own—if he has one— in exchange; but they are very averse to marrying one of their own relations—even of a distant degree. If a woman is supposed to have a child who is not her husband's, they consider it a great disgrace; and to the infant, death is almost certain. If again, a family increases too rapidly, for instance, if a woman has a child within twelve months of a previous one, they hold a consultation amongst the tribe she belongs to, as to whether it shall live or not; but if the father insists upon the life of the child being spared, they do not persist in its destruction, and especially if it is a female. At their confinements they receive no assistance whatever, but so soon as the child comes into the world, they wrap it up in a piece of skin rug; and, if on a journey, move on; it has no nourishment but the breast. They name them according to any circumstance that may happen; perhaps after the lake, or river they are near; or any accident or event which may have occurred—the whole family changing their names also, until another child is born—when they change again.

It will be seen by the foregoing, that jealousy is the prevalent cause of all their quarrels, for the women and the men are equally under the influences of the Green-eyed Monster. In the fights, however, which ensue, the poor women get much the worst of it, for after having had their furious combats amongst themselves, the husbands think it necessary to turn to also, and thrash them into quietude.

The meetings of different tribes, I found were not solely for the purposes of exchanging food, but for the very laudable purpose of *bringing out* their very elegant, amiable, marriageable daughters, to be seen and known, and of course, courted. By this very natural process, much ill-will and wild desperate passions are unfortunately excited—so that wounds, not only of the heart, but of the head, and frightful murders ensue; some of them never to be forgiven, until a fearful revenge has followed.

Previous to breaking up from our present ground there was another battle, so that when the other tribe left, one of ours stole after them in the night and speared a man dead, who was sleeping in his hut beside his wife; he sent his spear right through him into the ground, for no other cause than that the murdered man had promised him his daughter years before, and had then given her to another. Having had his revenge he returned, and boasted of what he had done, upon which his relations and particular friends left the place, apparently apprehending an attack. The next morning, those who remained went to the tribe to which the murdered man belonged, and found him rolled up in his rug, ready to be tied up in a tree—a mode of disposing of the dead, who were not enemies, unknown to me before. They selected a strong, if not a lofty tree, and in the branches, about twelve feet up, they placed some logs and branches across, and sheets of bark; on these they laid the body with the face upwards, inclining toward the setting sun, and over it was placed some more bark and boughs, and then logs as heavy as the branches would bear; all this being done to protect the body from the birds of prey. Whilst this was going on, the women sat round the tree joining with the widow in the most bitter lamentations, pitiable to hear. A fire was, as usual, made all round this extraordinary tomb, and at that side in particular which was nearest to the sun at its setting, so that he might have, in the morning, not only the sun's rays, but the fire to cheer and warm him. All things being completed, one word was uttered, 'anima-diate', which means, he is gone to be made a white man, but not for ever. The murdered man appeared to have been an especial favourite, and the mourning was long and very general. The hair of all was cut short with sharp shells—both men and women daubing themselves with clay, and the latter crying very lamentably throughout the night. I was much distressed at all this, for their grief was genuine, and the poor creatures had no Christian comfort or hope to fall back upon.

I suffered much mentally, so that I determined on once more attempting my escape, being sick at heart, and of these scenes altogether, for scarcely a month had passed without their being repeated. My guardians, or I may again say, my relations, according to their superstitious fashion, however assured me nothing should happen to me, under the circumstances by which I had *returned* amongst them.

After a long conversation, the following morning we parted with the other tribe, apparently on friendly terms, and at length joined the rest of our people who had left us, and having crossed the Barwin, had gone as far as a spot called Biarhoo, where we halted. Very angry discussions arose about the murdered man, and at one time it appeared that the savage who had slain him would be served in a similar manner; but after awhile we all moved on to a place they call Godocut, near the sea side, where we pitched our bark huts on a high projecting piece of land, from whence we could command an extensive view, so that no strangers could approach us unobserved. They evidently expected a hostile visit from some of the friends of the man who had been killed, and kept a good look-out for mischief. At this spot, however, nothing was to be had to eat but shell fish; so we soon left for another about eight miles distant, going through a very thick scrub to reach it, which occasioned me great pain—my trowsers being almost useless, and the skin rug being my only upper covering. Here we settled down for a few days, near two fresh water wells, hunting opossums and digging roots.

Our next journey was to Palac Palac, a halting place in some very extensive plains, with here and there a tree upon them, where we remained many months, there being plenty of animal food and a good deal of fish in the water holes.

Great anxiety was still felt about our safety, and watch was kept night and day, to prevent surprise. One day a numerous tribe was seen crossing the plains coming in our direction, and all our party took to their heels for the nearest shelter, where we remained all the night with nothing to eat, for the natives seldom provide for their wants beforehand. The next morning several of our people were sent out to reconnoitre, and not returning all that day and the next night, considerable apprehension was felt at their absence. The following day, however, they brought the satisfactory intelligence, that the party we had seen were not enemies, but part of a tribe with which we were on friendly terms, who had halted about thirteen miles on. Our messengers brought with them some fire-sticks, so that we were again able to make fires to cook our food—having, in our hasty flight, left ours behind us, at the place to which we now returned.

After some time, a messenger came to say the friendly tribe had found a great abundance of eels, in the lagoon near which they had encamped, and that they wished us to come and share in their good fortune. This is customary amongst those tribes who are friendly with each other; so we accepted the invitation and joined them that day. Being now in considerable strength, we did not fear attack, and it afterwards proved there was no occasion for apprehension, as the friends of the murdered native never sought revenge for the deed. Being in such excellent quarters, and in perfect safety—excepting occasional domestic quarrels—there was nothing to disturb the general tranquillity; and, consequently, I became daily more acquainted with their language and habits. By way of relieving the monotony of this narrative, I may as well, therefore, here relate a few particulars.

The natives inhabiting that part of the coast of New Holland, round Port Phillip, now known as the colony of Victoria, are generally of a middle stature, with a dark complexion; but not so dark as those of warmer latitudes. Their forms and features are not strikingly handsome certainly, but many of them would be good-looking, did they not make such horrid frights of themselves by plastering their hair and daubing their faces and bodies all over with pipe-clay and ochre. Their hair is not curly like the African, but straight, looking terribly unsentimental. In fact, every hair of the head appears to be deranged, or out of temper with its owner; and well it may be, for it gets frightfully cut and hacked about, sometimes by shells, and flints, and such like; besides being made the abode of certain living tormentors, which it would be unparliamentary to mention, or describe more particularly. They are not at all nice about their food; all kinds of beasts, and fish, and fowl, reptile, and creeping things—although when alive poisonous—being acceptable. It is quantity, not quality, with them.

They have no notion of a Supreme Being, although they have of an after life, as in my case; and they do not offer up any kind of prayer, even to the sun or moon, as is customary with most other uncivilized people. They have a notion, that the world is supported by props, which are in the charge of a man who lives at the farthest end of the earth. They were dreadfully alarmed on one occasion when I was with them, by news passed from tribe to tribe, that unless they could send him a supply of tomahawks for cutting some more props with, and some more rope to tie them with, the earth would go by the run, and all hands would be smothered. Fearful of this, they began to think, and enquire, and calculate, where the highest mountains were, and how to get at them, and on them, so as to have some chance of escape from the threatened danger. Notwithstanding this forethought, they set to work to provide the needful, and succeeded in this way. Passing on the word to the tribes along the coast, some settlers at a very great distance were robbed of axes, and saws, and rope, and tiers of dray wheels; all of which were forwarded on from tribe to tribe, to the old gentleman on the other side; and, as was supposed, in time to prevent the capsize, for it never happened. A tribute of this description is paid whenever possible; but who the knowing old juggling receiving thief is, I could never make out. However, it is only one of the same sort of robberies which are practised in the other countries of what is called Christendom; and as I have no particular wish to dwell upon them in this narrative, let us pass on.

Their notion of the origin of fire is this, that as a native woman was digging at an ant hill one day, for the purpose of getting their eggs for eating, a crow flying over her dropped something like dry grass, which immediately blazed, and set a tree on fire. For this reason, they very much respect the Waakee, as they call the bird, and do not kill and eat him, unless pressed by necessity.

I will now describe their war and hunting implements, and then continue my every day narrative of events.

The spear which they use, is from ten to fifteen feet long, and is made of a solid piece of wood, very sharp at the point—some having rows of teeth; these are called jagged spears, because they cannot be easily extracted from either man or beast. The natives call them Karnwell. There is also a smaller kind, the Daar spear, used in hunting; it is made of two pieces of wood, fastened together with the sinews of the kangaroo. They are very sharp at the point, and have a white flint stone on each side, fastened in, and on, with gum. These they throw an amazing distance and with great force, seldom missing their aim at a kangaroo when bounding past at full speed, and at fifty paces distance. There is also another kind of spear but it is chiefly used in warfare; it is a very dry piece of wood inserted into a piece of strong reed; it, altogether, being nearly seven feet long, and bound together by the sinews of the kangaroo. They have another instrument called the marriwan, having at the smaller end a sort of hook. The boomerang, or wangaam, as they are called, is made from a solid piece of wood formed in the shape of a half-moon; this they hurl at their antagonists with great force, holding it at one end before letting it go spinning against the enemy. They have a kind of shield also made of wood, a broad solid piece of about three feet long, tapering at each end, with a handle cut in the side, so as to admit the hand. These shields, which they call malka, are used very dexterously in warding off spears and blows from the waddie, or koor, a piece of wood very much resembling a cricket bat. And then there is the jeangwell, another piece of wood cut into a half-square at one end, with a handle to it and a knob at the end. These two war weapons are excellent at close quarters.

Now readers, let us go back to the plain where I said we were living in peace and with great abundance of food for many months; of course, travelling about that particular locality occasionally as it suited our purposes, either for hunting, or for mere pleasure.

Getting tired at length of the sameness of food, we all left and travelled about twenty miles, as I suppose, into the bush, to a place called Boordek, where opossums were plentiful. My brother-in-law, as he considered himself to be, had shown me how to ascertain when these animals were up the trees, and how the natives took them; this was, in the first place, by breathing hard on the bark, so as to discover if there was any opossum hairs left attached to it when the animal ascended. This found, he next cut a notch in the bark with his tomahawk, in which to insert his toe, and then another notch, holding the tomahawk in his mouth after making the incision, and so on upwards; by this means climbing the highest trees, and dragging the animals out of their holes, and off the branches by their legs and tails, and then throwing them down to me at the foot; my business being to kill, and carry them. At the former I was tolerably expert, so that he often cried out from aloft, Merrijig; which means well done. We lived in clover at this place, getting plenty of opossums, and a very excellent root, which, when roasted, I found as sweet as a chestnut, and as white as flour.

Our next halting place was Morriock, where we found a great abundance of squirrels.[1] After being there some time, the greater part of the men left on a distant hunting excursion, leaving about half-a-dozen other men and myself in charge of the women and children. On going away, they marked their arms in the usual manner with stripes, to denote how many days they would be absent; and one man of ours, who remained, did the same; rubbing off one mark each day, to denote the lapse of time. Soon after our people had left, another tribe came and made their huts very near to ours. The very next day they began to show hostile intentions, taking advantage of our weakness, and at length threw their spears, killing a boy and girl. Upon this a conflict ensued, which lasted about an hour. Finding we could defend ourselves, they very soon left, and we immediately sent away a messenger to our tribe to tell them what had happened in their absence. They returned as quickly as possible, and a war council was held as to the propriety of following the others, which ended in preparations being made for a pursuit. The smearing with pipe-clay began again, and the spears and other implements were made ready for action.

It appeared the cause of their attack upon us was some very old grievance about the women. I am sorry to say it, but these dear creatures were at the bottom of every mischief. From Adam, that old root digger, downwards, it has always been the same, in every clime, and nation.—Then why fancy my very pretty looking, slightly clad Venuses, to be worse than others?—On their part, I repudiate the imputation.

The next morning our party started, fully armed for the combat, and with passions highly excited at the thought of the advantage taken of them by their cowardly assailants. After they were gone, we, who were left, buried the bodies of the children in the usual manner. After two days' absence, our fighting men returned, several of them severely wounded; but their revenge was satisfied, for they had killed two of their opponents.

The next place we went to was called Ballackillock, where we found a tribe already settled, if a few days' residence under sheets of bark and branches of trees, may be so called. Both parties were very friendly for a short time, and then there was a great fight, in which a young woman, about twenty years of age, was speared through the thigh. As she belonged to our tribe, she was brought into our huts, from whence it seemed, she had absconded with a man of the other party, without her parents' knowledge. The quarrel being over, and all quiet, the men went to the lake fishing, leaving the women to their usual occupation, and the poor girl by herself in one of the huts. The man she had eloped with knowing all this, went to her, and carried her off; so that when the tribe returned they discovered the flight of the fugitives, on whom they vowed vengeance. All went on as usual for a few days more, and then we shifted again, and for some time kept moving about, killing squirrels and opossums—the skins of both being very much estimated. There is another kind of animal the natives kill and eat—it is called the karbor, about the size of a dog—thick and short in the body, with a tremendous large head, and very short legs, armed with claws covered over with thick frizzly hair of a light brown colour; they inhabit the branches of high trees in the day, but at night they descend to eat the grass, and roots, these being their principal food.[2] When wounded they make the most pitiable cries, like those of young children in pain; they make the same noise in the night; and many a time have they kept me awake whilst on my lonely wanderings.[3] They are very harmless, making no resistance when taken, might be easily domesticated, are excellent eating, and very much resembling pork in flavour. They carry their young in a pouch under the belly the same as the kangaroo; and, notwithstanding their singular and somewhat unwieldy appearance, are very active, springing from branch to branch, like squirrels.

We now started to meet, by invitation, another tribe who were halted near a small stream running into the Barwin. The second day, we reached the appointed place, which the natives call Monwak, but they were not there; so we sent off a messenger to inform them of our approach; at length we found them, in great strength, smearing themselves all over with clay, and apparently preparing for some important occasion. On learning this, our tribe did the same, jumping about as if mad. In the afternoon the others arrived, with the man who had run away with the girl of our tribe at their head; the whole body following him in something like close column, so that I saw clearly there would be another battle.

In the first place, they seated themselves on their rugs, in groups of half-dozens, or thereabouts, keeping their spears, and shields, and waddies all ready at hand; our party being prepared also. At length the young man already mentioned, advanced towards us. He had bunches of emu's feathers tied to different parts of his body by a kind of yarn they make by twisting the hair of the opossum; he was cutting the most extraordinary capers, and challenged our men to fight—an offer which was accepted practically—by a boomerang being thrown at him, and which grazed his leg. A spear was then thrown, but he warded it off cleverly with his shield. He made no return to this, but kept capering and jumping about, until one of our men advanced very near to him, with only a shield and a waddie, and then the two went to work in good earnest, blow following blow, until the first had his shield split, so that he had nothing to defend himself with but his waddie. His opponent took advantage of this, and struck him a tremendous blow on one side of the head, and knocked him down; but he was instantly on his legs again, the blood however flowing very freely over his back and shoulders. His friends then cried out enough, and threatened general hostilities if another blow was struck; and this having the desired effect, they all, soon after, separated quietly, thus ending an affair which at one time promised to conclude very differently.

The next day we moved on to another fresh water lake of considerable extent, where we encamped, not very much at our ease, as we saw another tribe on the opposite shore. In the middle of the night we heard a dreadful uproar in that direction, and in the morning learned that those we had seen before dark had been fallen upon by some others whilst they were sleeping; so on hearing this we went to their assistance. On our arrival a horrid scene presented itself, many women and children laying about in all directions, wounded and sadly mutilated. Several of the poor creatures had rushed into the lake and were drowned. The few who had escaped were hiding themselves in the reeds; but on our proffering assistance and protection, they joined us, and went to our huts. The dead were left, it not being safe to lose time in burying them, as our number was not sufficient to make us safe from a similar attack. The day following we therefore left the spot, and kept wandering about for some time after, until we came again to our old quarters at Moodewari, where we remained some months.

Having come to another halt, the better way perhaps will be, for me here to state, that the tribes are divided into families; or rather, I should say, composed of them—each tribe comprising from twenty to sixty of them. They acknowledge no particular Chief as being superior to the rest; but, he who is most skilful and useful to the general community, is looked upon with the greatest esteem, and is considered to be entitled to more wives than any of the others. They contrive to keep a tolerable account, by recollection, of their pedigree, and will not, as I observed before, knowingly marry a relation —except where two brothers happened to be married, and one dies; in that case the survivor claims the widow; in fact, as many wives or widows as he has left behind him. Should the women object, there is little chance of their lives being spared, as this law of custom is absolute. They are in general, very kind to their children, excepting the child is from any cause, believed to be illegitimate; and again, when a woman has been promised to one man, and is afterwards given to another; in such case, her first-born is almost invariably killed at its birth. The tribes would be much more numerous were it not for these barbarous and inhuman sacrifices.

As soon as the children are able to toddle about, they begin, as if by instinct, to search for food, and at four or five years of age, are able to dig roots and live without the aid of their parents; to whom, as may be supposed, their drapery, and washing and combing, etc., is no sort of trouble. They are all stark naked, and tumble about in the lagoons and rivers, like so many jolly young porpoises playing in the sun.

They have a brutal aversion to children who happen to be deformed at their birth. I saw the brains of one dashed out at a blow, and a boy belonging to the same woman made to eat the mangled remains. The act of cannibalism was accounted for in this way. The woman at particular seasons of the moon, was out of her senses; the moon—as they thought—having affected the child also; and, certainly, it had a very singular appearance. This caused her husband to deny his being the father, and the reason given for making the boy eat the child was, that some evil would befall him if he had not done so.

1. Probably gliding possums.
2. This is a rather garbled account of the koala, which was evidently then a rare species. Some elements, such as the grass eating and the flavour of its flesh, are more consistent with the wombat.
3. This may be the call of a gliding possum.

CHAPTER V

Ev'n the low hut—poor shelter—while he slept
Shook in the earthquake, or the storm, or the rain:
Thus, sick at heart, the Exile stood and wept,
O'er thought and care, and hope and toil, in vain

Having told this horrible tale, let us now return to our halting place at Moodiwiri, when, after a long time another tribe joined us, and a dispute arose about surrendering a woman who had been carried away. The man who had her with him refused to give her up, so she was forcibly taken from him and brought to the hut I was in, very much to my dissatisfaction. I was greatly annoyed at it, because I thought the matter would not end there, and so it turned out; for when the native from whom she had been taken, found she was gone, he resolved on vengeance, and with this view, when we were all asleep, he came to our hut and speared the man of whom he was jealous. He pierced him to the ground, right through his body. Hearing the noise occasioned by this assault, I gave the alarm, but he was gone, taking with him the woman. The poor fellow's brother who was wounded, and myself, endeavoured to draw the spear, but could not, even by twisting it round, it being jagged; at length a woman succeeded, but although everything was done to save him, he died in a very few hours. The next day he was buried, or rather suspended on the branches of a tree as before described, his mother making horrible lamentations, and burning her body all over with fire-sticks. The next day the men set off to find the murderer, but not succeeding, they returned a little before dark.

A short time after this affair we shifted our quarters, and, when on a hunting excursion, accidentally fell in with the tribe to which he belonged, and a very desperate fight ensued. As is the case with them in such matters, when the parents cannot be punished for any wrong done, they inflict it upon the offspring. So now, the savages having got hold of a child of about four years of age, which this man had had by the young woman before referred to, they immediately knocked it on the head, and having destroyed it, they killed the murderer's brother, also spearing his mother through the thigh, and wounding at the same time several others; so that vengeance was heaped upon him and his tribe in a most dreadful manner. However, the man himself having escaped, he, with others, went in the night to the hut of the savage who had killed his brother, and speared him dead; having done which, they cut the most of the flesh off his body, carrying it away on their spears to mark their triumph. The next day and night there was a continued uproar of dancing and singing, to notify their joy at these horrible events; during which, the mangled remains of the man were roasted between heated stones—and they eat part of them, and no mistake; for I saw them join in the horrible repast, and was requested to do so likewise, which of course I refused to do, evincing the greatest disgust at their proceedings.

Having been rescued from death by starvation, it is only natural that I should, from a feeling of gratitude, desire to save the natives from so great a reproach; but the truth must prevail, and that many of the natives inhabiting this part of the continent of New Holland are cannibals, under particular circumstances, cannot be doubted.

During their savage and brutal repast, I was told it was their intention to serve every one of the murderer's tribe in the same manner.

After this affair, we continued wandering about in a similar way, from place to place, joining one tribe, then leaving it for another, and so on, nothing particular occurring. At length we pitched our huts upon the borders of a lake or lagoon, with a long name, it being called Koodgingmurrah, the name they give to a root growing thereabouts. At that place another tribe joined us, and in a very few days another skirmish took place, and, as usual, it was all about the women. In this fight I was very nearly killed by a boomerang, which split my shield in two. It appeared not to have been intended for me, but for my supposed brother-in-law. The man, in spite of my intercession, was punished very severely for having thrown it; for which, however, he professed great sorrow. Having been slightly wounded in the hand, and the blood flowing, the women came crying, and bound it up with a piece of rug, tying it round with oppossum sinews. The next morning we went to the other side of the lake, where we remained many months.

Another halt—let me then make the best of it, by relating something more about the habits of my Aboriginal friends: the wild uncivilized inhabitants of the forest, the uncultivated children of nature; thousands of whom live unknown, and die unpitied.

All those I met with, excepting in times of war, or lamentation, I found to be particularly fond of what they consider music, although they have no kind of instrument except the skin rug, which, stretched from knee to knee, they beat upon, others keeping time with sticks. So passionately attached are they even to this noise, that they often commence in the night, one family setting them on, until at last they one and all become a very jolly set, keeping it up in one continual strain until daylight. I have often wished them and their enchanting enlivening strains on the other side of the Continent, with the queer old conjuror who manages the props already mentioned, to whom I must however avoid alluding more particularly.

They have a great aversion to the use of water, unless for the purposes of drinking, and bathing in the summer season, so that their washing processes are not very laborious or extensive. Nature, as it is, reigns in all her glory with them, without artificial assistance. My gentlemen, and lady friends, as may be supposed, knew nothing about tailors, and dressmakers, hairdressers, or boot and shoe makers; they were as ignorant in all such matters as Eve or Adam. They, however, take great pains in greasing and painting themselves in the most fantastic manner. Their style of shaving is not the most agreeable, for when the beard is nearly full grown they singe it with a fire-stick, or pluck it off with a muscle-shell. They have a great aversion to grey hairs, whether in the head or beard. The women pluck them out whenever they appear on their husbands or their own heads, until old father Time gets the better of them at that work. They are very fond of ornaments—the women especially—and in their manufacture, are very ingenious. Their head-bands are netted like silk purses, and they do this kind of work without any needle or other instrument—using their fingers only. They make these bands as even as it could be done by the most experienced person with silk or thread, leaving a piece at each end to tie round the forehead, colouring them with ochre. Their neck ornaments are made like silk velvet guards. Upon these are strung a great number of pieces of shells, and of the teeth of the kangaroo, adding too, the feathers of the swan and emu; the strongest of which they split in the middle, in order to make them more pliable. Many of the women have rings made out of the bones of birds suspended from the inside of their nostrils, and the men have a small straight bone with a sort of knob at one end. Those who have the most ornaments are considered the most fashionable and attractive.

The baskets I mentioned before are made of rushes and grass, dried and split; and so nicely are they turned out of hand, as to have the appearance of those manufactured in India; but they are much more durable. No person could suppose they were the handywork of an uncivilized people. To return.

We remained at the opposite side of the lake, until the approach of spring. Here they made their food principally of the large ants called the kalkeeth, which are found in hives within hollow trees.[1] In order to ascertain where they are, the trees are struck with the tomahawk, and, at the noise, they show themselves at the holes. An entrance for the hand is then made, and so they are taken out and put into baskets, being, at the proper season, as fat as marrow. These creatures are prepared for eating, by placing them on slips of bark about three feet long and one foot wide, and so, burnt, or roasted. It is only for about one month in each year they can be had, for after that time they are transformed to large flies, and then fly away to die, or again change their shape and nature.

Having finished this ant hunting and eating expedition, we shifted our quarters; but before I go any further I must say something about their tomahawk; which, perhaps, as a very important instrument, ought to have been mentioned in an earlier part of this narrative. The heads of these instruments are made from a hard black stone, split into a convenient thickness, without much regard to shape. This they rub with a very rough granite stone, until is it brought to a fine thin edge, and so hard and sharp as to enable them to fall a very large tree with it. There is only one place that I ever heard of in that country, where this hard and splitting stone is to be had. The natives call it karkeen; and say, that it is at a distance of three hundred miles from the coast, inland.[2] The journey to fetch them is, therefore, one of great danger and difficulty; the tribes who inhabit the immediate localities being very savage, and hostile to all others. I was told, that it required an armed party of resolute fighting men, to obtain supplies of this very necessary article; so that the tomahawk is considered valuable for all purposes. They vary in weight from four to fourteen pounds; the handles being thick pieces of wood split, and then doubled up, the stone being in the bend, and fixed with gum, very carefully prepared for the purpose, so as to make it perfectly secure when bound round with sinews.

A messenger now came from another tribe, to tell us they would be glad to see our party near a river they called Booneawillock—so named from a sort of eels they call Boonea—with which that stream abounds. It was very much swollen, in consequence of heavy floods, so that we could not cross it, to join our friends; we therefore pitched our huts on the other side. Many parts of that river are rocky, leaving but an inconsiderable depth of water, into which the eels get in great numbers; indeed so numerous were they, that we caught them in dozens. These eels appeared to be very sagacious, but not so much so as to avoid our fishing parties; for although they would shoot away into deep water at the falling of a star, or any extraordinary noise, yet they would come to our fishing torches and allow themselves to be taken very placidly.

When the flood in the river—which had been occasioned by very heavy and continuous rains—had subsided, we passed over, and hutted ourselves on the other side. Another tribe soon after joined us, amounting to about one hundred men, women, and children. I should here say, that the eels mentioned, seemed inexhaustible at this place, those of the smallest kind being the most numerous. They are light blue on the back, with white bellies; these the natives call the Mordong; and the larger kind, the Babbanien; the latter being brown on the back, with white bellies.

The tribe which arrived the last, only remained a few days, when another fight occurred, again about the women—one of whom was killed, and several severely wounded: they then left. We also shifted our quarters a short time after, and kept up the old fancy of wandering about; not exactly from 'post to pillar', but from one hunting ground to another, seeking variety of food, from fish to flesh, from roots to anything available; for the natives are, in truth, a rambling lot, never content—unless sleeping, and then dreaming of Corrobberrees, and fights, and mischief. In one of these excursions, one of our men was bitten by a snake whilst stepping over a fallen tree, of which bite the poor fellow died immediately. As he was one of the principal men of the tribe, his death caused great sorrow, and he was buried; or, rather stowed away in the branches of a very high tree, with all the honours suited to his value, as one of this very estimable community, of which I had, involuntarily, become a member.

Time passed on, and a variety of circumstances occurred to separate us, so that I was at last left with my supposed relations, and only two or three other families—each living in our separate huts.

One day we saw a large party of natives coming towards us, but they passed on to the back, at a distance;

and, when there, began to polish themselves up with clay, and ochre, as if for a fight; it occasioned us great alarm; but we hoped our defenceless position would induce them to treat us mercifully. There were about sixty of them, and they soon undeceived us as to their intentions; for they came first to the other bank of the river, shaking their spears; and then crossing over, attacked us so furiously, as to give the women and children only time to attempt escape. My old friend, and supposed brother-in-law, had a spear sent right through his body, and then they hunted out his wife and killed her dead upon the spot. The savages then came back to where I was supporting my wounded friend; who, seeing them approaching, sprung up, even in the last agonies of death, and speared the nearest assailant in the arm. My friend was, of course, dispatched immediately, with spears and boomerangs; as was a son of his, who was with us at the time. Strange to say, not one raised his hand against me; had I done so against them, I must have been sacrificed instantly; for what could I do, being only one against so many?

The cause of this sudden unprovoked cruelty was not, as usual, about the women, but because the man who had been killed by the bite of the snake belonged to the hostile tribe, and they believed my supposed brother-in-law carried about with him something that had occasioned his death. They have all sorts of fancies of this kind, and it is frequently the case, that they take a man's kidneys out after death, tie them up in something, and carry them round the neck, as a sort of protection and valuable charm, for either good or evil. They took the son's life because he had a daughter, who he had promised to the man who killed him, and had afterwards given her to another.

I should have been most brutally unfeeling, had I not suffered the deepest mental anguish from the loss of these poor people, who had all along been so kind and good to me. I am not ashamed to say, that for several hours my tears flowed in torrents, and, that for a long time I wept unceasingly. To them, as I have said before, I was as a living dead brother, whose presence and safety was their sole anxiety. Nothing could exceed the kindness these poor natives had shown me, and now they were dead, murdered by the band of savages I saw around me, apparently thirsting for more blood. Of all my sufferings in the wilderness, there was nothing equal to the agony I now endured. My feelings made me desperate, so that when a tall powerful fellow came to the hut some time after, to demand my friend's spears, I refused, in fierce language, to surrender them, so that he desisted; ordering me however away, with a quantity of fish, and his rug, to where his wife and family were, telling me to wait there until his arrival; at the same time, assuring me of his good-will and future friendship. These I did not choose to rely upon, and so, after having arrived at a convenient distance from the scene of these savage murders, I resolved on making my escape. With this view, I tied my spears together, and put myself in light marching order, rolled up my rug as tightly as possible, crossed the river, and made for the bush; going in another direction to that which I thought it likely the savages would follow in pursuit.

After what I have stated as to their cold-blooded murders, I may surely call them savages, although, as we have seen, there are many kind-hearted creatures amongst them.

When I got about four miles, I unexpectedly fell in with a tribe I knew, to whom, my hurry and fright was a source of great anxiety. I told them all that had happened, on hearing which, they immediately prepared for vengeance on the murderers for the young man was amongst them to whom my old friend's son had given the girl, instead of the man who had so barbarously murdered their father. Before they set off, they directed me where I should find them after the expedition they were going upon was over; so I started for the place appointed, near the Barwin River. The next day I swam across that river; taking with me my spears, and rugs, and fire-stick, and before night, set up my hut in a place from whence I could view the country all round. Before I lighted the fire, I made a turf and bark fence all about where it was to be, so that the flame should not be seen, for I was naturally in great dread of being overtaken. In this way I lived a few days, waiting for my friends. At length, one evening, I saw a light coming across the plain in my direction. This occasioned me great alarm, as I did not suppose the friendly tribe would travel in the night; so I put my fire out, hid my spears and fish, and concealed myself amongst the high reeds growing in the neighbourhood. After a time I heard female voices, and then one of them say, 'where can he be gone?' some surmising one cause, and some another, for my absence. This satisfied me that all was right, so I approached, agreeably surprising them by my appearance. They were five young women belonging to the last party we had met with, who had made their escape, in consequence of another great fight which had ensued between my old friends, and the tribe who had killed my protectors. They told me, three men of the hostile party had been killed, and that they had burned the bodies of my said-to-be brother-in-law, his wife, and his son, to prevent their enemies from mangling them; and, that if the women had not left, they would have been taken away by force by the opposite party. They, poor creatures, were dreadfully hungry and fatigued; so I gave them all the food I had and kept them in my hut until the morning, when two of them left, the other three remaining for several days longer, waiting for their friends. Finding they did not come, according to their appointment, they then went away also.

Having reason to think something had occurred to prevent their arrival, I returned to the scene of the brutal massacre; and finding the ashes and bones of my late friends, I scraped them up together, and covered them over with turf, burying them in the best manner I could, that being the only return I could make for their many kindnesses. I did so in great grief at the recollection of what they had done for me through so many years, and in all my dangers and troubles.

My next move was back again to the hut I had left on the plains where the women had found me, and the following day the others came according to their promise. They endeavoured to persuade me to join them permanently, saying they would protect me; that, as I was alone I should certainly be killed; but I refused, having no faith in their professions, and being sick at heart, so shortly after witnessing all these atrocities. After staying a short time at this spot, they left me, crossing over the river, and when they were out of sight, I packed up my traps, and started in an opposite direction, going towards the sea. When at a place called Mangawhawz, where there was a well of fresh water and plenty of all kinds of fish, I put up a hut, and remained there several months alone. I had now passed so many years in this sort of way—more I should think than five-and-twenty—and had got so much accustomed to the kind of life, as to have forgotten the use of my own language, and began to be careless about every thing civilized, fancying I could never return to a better kind of existence, or to the intercourse of any other society than that of the tribes, if I was again forced into communication with them. I had ascertained from the natives long before, that the *Calcutta* had left the bay, and that the first settlement had been abandoned. I often looked towards the sea, thinking I might observe some vessel passing; but no, not one; for at that time there was little voyaging round the coast,—South Australia, and the other settlements, not having been formed, and ships from Sydney keeping well off the land, few of them passing through the Straits at any time. Although so desolately placed, I, for a long time, fancied myself comparatively happy, and that I could gladly have ended my days there. If I had had books they would have been totally useless, having forgotten all the little knowledge I had learned in my early days; therefore I could only seek my food—eat, drink, and sleep; but how I could have passed so long a time in such a way, is to me now a matter of bewildering astonishment. It is related in the fabulous history of Robinson Crusoe, that he was fortunate enough to save a Bible from the wreck of his ship, and by that means consoled and benefited himself; but I, the real Crusoe, for so many years amongst savages, in the then unknown forests and wilds of the vast Australian Continent, had no such help to my mind, and I beg the humane reader to reflect on this circumstance with feelings of kindly sympathy—for mine was, in truth, a sad existence. I was indeed a lone man, without any other resource than an entire reliance upon the great God, who had so wonderfully preserved me; and to whom, I say again, I did not forget to pray earnestly and fervently, for health, sustenance, and protection.

1. Termites.
2. Probably Mt William near Lancefield.

CHAPTER VI

The breeze came gently o'er me from the west,
Where the last sunbeams linger e'er they part;
Along the beach I lay, to sleep, and rest,
My wearied limbs, and still more wearied heart

At length I was compelled to leave my quarters and move to the Karaaf River again, where I built a more substantial hut, the locality being full of roots. Unfortunately I had no dog to hunt the kangaroo, so my dependence was chiefly upon the fish, which sometimes however, were very scarce. Before I made this change of quarters the winter had set in very tempestuously, and I suffered very much from the cold weather and continued rains. One day, whilst watching the fish, I saw a great shoal of bream come into the mouth of the river, making their way up a long distance, to a bend where it branches off, and where it is of considerable depth. When the tide turned, they came down with it again, and it occurred to me that if I could by any means stop them in their retreat by a sort of wear, I should have a great supply of food, thus placed at my command, as it would seem, by Providence; so I turned my thoughts to this all that day, and all night long. After examining the river, I found a spot suited to the purpose, where the tide did not rise above two feet, and here I resolved on making the attempt. With this view, I set to work making faggots with rushes and boughs of trees—carrying them down to the bank of the river; and at the same time, preparing long stakes, sharpened at one end, to make them fast in the sand. At length I had a sufficient number together to commence operations, and taking advantage of the tide when it receded, I set about my undertaking, and completed a wear,[1] working incessantly; so that when the fish came down with the stream in thousands, they found themselves intercepted, and being apparently confounded at this, they turned tail up again, and then down, and so on; but by that time the top of my wear was above the surface, and they were obliged to surrender at discretion. I caught in this way, considerable numbers, and consequently was in great delight; for with them, and the roots growing thereabout, I had food in abundance. I gathered—or rather caught, I should say— heaps of them, and employed myself in drying and preserving them—many of these fish weighing three pounds each and more—being also of very delicious flavour. With feelings of comparative content, I set about improving my habitation, making it more substantial and comfortable, by getting some logs, and making the roof better able to resist the cold and rains. The branches of trees and their supporters I covered with turf, making the sides of that material, forming a chimney of the same; so that after a few days' labour, I found myself more at home in my solitary abode, having from the doorway a long view over the plain, and out to sea.

It was necessary, I found, to consult the moon, so as to judge of the ebbing and flowing of the tides; for the fish, I ascertained came and went accordingly; and therefore, in order to prevent a scarcity, it was proper I should dry them in the sun, by spreading them about on the trees, and on the roof of my hut, taking them inside on every appearance of rain, or other unfavourable weather. There was another sort of food very useful to me; this was a particular kind of root the natives call Murning—in shape, and size, and flavour, very much resembling the radish.

Whilst employed with my fish one day. I heard voices near me. One said 'Amadeat', meaning, white man. The first thing to be done was to conceal myself; but presently I saw two men, and two women, with several children. One of them called out, in their language, 'It is me,' meaning by that, they were friends, and that I need not be alarmed. I soon found they belonged to the tribe of my old friend: my tribe, I may say. On seeing me, the women began to cry with joy at finding me safe. It was more than a year, perhaps nearly two, since I had met them, or any human being; and they supposed me to have been killed long since. One of the men took a leg of kangaroo out of his basket, and some of the roots and gum they had, and gave them to me; and in return, I took them to my hut and offered them fish, of which food I showed them my great abundance, and told them my adventures since we parted; at which they expressed much delight, singing and capering about in a most wild and extravagant manner.

When I explained my plan of entrapping the fish, they could not contain themselves for joy, patting me on the back, and saying I deserved three or four wives for my invention. For some cause or other they then told their women to go away; they, however, would not, but began stamping and beating the ground, expressive of their dissatisfaction. After a time the men went off to spear fish, and on their return they set up their huts near mine, and so made themselves comfortable for many days. After a time they persuaded me to accompany them to a salt lake, called Nellemengobeet, about five miles off, which lake is only separated from the sea by a narrow belt, or sand-bank. Near it was a well of very good water, and there we encamped, our object being to gather gum and roots.

When the moon was again at the full we returned to the Karaaf—my old fishing quarters; where our success was so great, that one of the party went away to fetch the remainder of the tribe, to share with us in kindness our abundant supplies. They soon joined us, bringing with them a quantity of kangaroo; and seeing we were so comfortable, they pitched their huts beside our party.

Having heard of the massacre of my friends, they vowed vengeance against the murderers; but the resources of food I had provided by means of the wears, being so ample, they remained content for a long time, heaping upon me all the civilities possible, for having put them in the way of procuring fish for themselves and families so easily.

After some time, we all went away together in search of the kangaroo, of which we killed a great many, as also of the norngnor—an animal about the size of a small pig. It is the creature the English call the wombat. They live in holes in the earth, of about twenty feet long and from ten to twenty deep, in an oblique direction, burrowing in them like the mole. When well cooked, they are good eating. The mouth of this creature is furnished with large teeth, their ears scarcely discernable, their legs being very short and armed with long claws; the skin is very tough, with short hair upon it, but they are without tails. The wombats feed on grass chiefly, only venturing out after dark, or on moonlight nights, returning to their burrows at day-break. The natives take these creatures by sending a boy or girl into their burrows, which they enter feet first, creeping in backwards until they touch the animal. Having discovered the lair, they call out as loud as they can, beating the ground over head, whilst those above are carefully listening—their ears being pressed close to the earth. By this plan of operations, they are enabled to tell with great precision the spot where they are. A perpendicular hole is then made, so as to strike the extremity of the burrow: and having done this, they dig away with sharp sticks, lifting the mould out in baskets. The poor things are easily killed, for they offer no resistance to these intrusions on their haunts. There is, however, a good deal of difficulty in making these holes, and in getting down so deep to them—so that it is a sort of hunting for food, of which the natives are not very fond. Except when the wombat has young, it is seldom that more than one is found in a hole. The animal is generally roasted whole, after having had the entrails taken out, which is all the preparation—the fire doing all the rest. And whilst alluding to this method of cookery, I may as well state, that in summer fire is very easily obtained by rubbing together two sticks of the wood they call Dealwark. They sometimes carry these unlighted fire-sticks about with them, wrapped up in a sort of covering made of opossum hair. In the winter months they are often very much distressed for fire, and suffer greatly from hunger and cold; their only covering being skin rugs, sewn together with sinews—using as needles fine bones of the kangaroo. These rugs serve them also to lay upon. Considering how they are exposed to the weather, it is wonderful how little they suffer from idleness;[2] for, excepting a sort of erysipelas, or scurvy, with which they are sometimes afflicted, they are in general very healthy. I never observed any European contagious disease prevalent, in the least degree; and this I thought strange. There was at one time however, I now recollect, a complaint which spread through the country, occasioning the loss of many lives, attacking generally the healthiest and strongest, whom it appeared to fix upon in preference to the more weakly. It was a dreadful swelling of the feet, so that they were unable to move about, being also afflicted with ulcers of a very painful kind.

I may as well here also mention a curious custom they have relative to their domestic affairs—if such a term can be applied to such a people. In many instances, a girl, almost as soon as she is born, is given to a man. After this promise, the mother of the child never again voluntarily speaks to the intended husband before he takes her to himself, nor to any of his brothers, if he has any; on the contrary she shuns them in the most careful manner. If the future son-in-law, or either of his brothers, should visit the tribe, she is always previously informed of his coming, so that she may have time to get out of the way; and if by chance she meets them, she covers her head over with her skin cloak. If any present is sent to her, such as opossum or kangaroo, and such like food, the receivers rub their faces and hands over with charcoal before it is taken and tasted. When again, a present of a skin cloak is made by the intended son-in-law, the mother gives it to her husband to wear for some time before it is favoured with her acceptance. This practice is adhered to on both sides, for the son-in-law may see his proposed father, but will not on any account see the mother; their notions on these matters being, that when their children are married the parents become much older, and if the girl's mother happens to see the proposed husband it will cause her hair to turn grey immediately.

To return to my narrative. We remained for a very long time at this place, and were ultimately joined by two tribes, one being called the Putnaroo, the other the Warwaroo, who usually inhabited the opposite side of the bay, a long way off, and on this occasion had left their women and children behind them. Having erected their bark huts near ours, they remained peaceable enough for several days, hunting and enjoying themselves; at length, the Putnaroos suddenly surrounded our people, and without any previous altercation speared a young man about twenty years of age. The cause stated to be was, that the murdered man had been promised a girl who his assailant wanted for himself.

No mother-in-law for awhile — what a deal.

Poor fellow, when he was speared, he ran only a very few paces, and then dropped down dead. Our tribe expostulated with the others against this assault, but were answered by the threat, that if they said much about it they would serve us in a similar manner; so we, being by far the weaker party, were obliged to appear to be satisfied.

This affair broke up our encampment, and I was sent to inform the friends of the deceased of what had happened, and also to watch the movements of the Putnaroos. Having found all this out, namely, where the enemy were, and the young man's parents, I made the latter acquainted with the circumstances connected with his death; telling them at the same time, that his remains had been deposited in the branch of a tree; which news gladdened them much, for in the first place they imagined the savages had taken his body away. When they had consoled themselves a little, the father summoned all the tribe and other friends he could muster; they came in considerable force, and having pipe-clayed and ochred themselves all over, they set off, prepared for battle. This however was evaded, as the Putnaroo invaders had taken to their heels, on seeing the great numbers to which they were opposed.

We now took up our quarters at a place they called Nullemungobeed, situated in the centre of a very extensive plain, with wells of good water handy. When we had settled ourselves down there, some of the men went to the spot where we had left the young man's remains hanging in the tree, and brought away the lower part of the body, leaving the upper quarters and head where they found it suspended. The usual uproar commenced amongst the women on the arrival of the part of the corpse, lamentation succeeding lamentation, burning with fire-sticks, and all the rest of it, until at length the mangled remains were roasted between heated stones, shared out, and greedily devoured by these savages. Again I was pressed to join in this horrid repast; but I hope I need not say, that I refused, with indignation and disgust.

Strange as all these cannibal ceremonies may appear, it is proper to explain, that many are performed out of what they consider respect for the deceased; the cap bones of whose knees, in this instance, after being carefully cleaned, were tied up in a sort of net of hair and twisted bark. Under such circumstances, these relics are carried by the mothers, tied round their necks by day, and placed under their heads by night, as affectionate remembrancers of the dead.

Being again thoroughly disgusted with these inhuman scenes, I went away alone, back to my old hut at the Karaaf River, where I fished as before by means of my wear, and lived for many months, daily expecting a visit from some of the tribes; but, by their absence, they all appeared to have deserted me. One day, however, a friendly party visited my solitary abode, and settled themselves down. In this way we all lived on for several months more, having plenty of fish and roots.

And now, reader, I come to a very important period of my life, which was a decision arrived at by my friends that I should take unto myself a wife. I was not in any way consulted, being considered a sort of instrument in their hands to do with as they might think proper. My wife was a young widow, about twenty years of age, tolerably good-looking, after a fashion, and apparently very mild tempered. The marriage feast, the ring, the fees for the ceremony, the bride's dress, my own, and all the rest of it, did not cost much. I was not obliged to run in debt, or fork out every shilling, or pay fifty per cent for discounting a bill to pay the piper—nothing of the kind; so I took her to myself, to my turf and bark hunting and fishing hut, on the banks of the Karaaf River.—I should here mention, that although previously married, my wife did not present me, on the day of our union, with any tender little remembrances of her first husband, my predecessor in her affections. Affections!— we shall see more about that presently; but, perhaps I may as well say at once, that my dearly beloved played me most abominably false, for at the end of our honeymoon, (perhaps it might have been a few months after *that* moon had gone down) one evening when we were alone in our hut, enjoying our domestic felicity, several men came in, and took her away from me by force; she, however, going very willingly. The next day—as I had no Supreme Court to go to for damages—I went over to the tribe the intruders belonged to, and told them how I had been treated. I confess I did not make a very great fuss about my loss—if it was one—but endeavoured to whistle it down the wind gaily. Several of the friendly natives were anxious I should take the usual revenge upon her and the man she had left me to live with, but I refused, and in the end, she was speared by another man, with whom she had been coqueting, and to whom she had also played falsely. Mixed up by relationship, as all these parties were, after a great number of altercations about her having run away from me, and the circumstances of her death, there was another fight, in which many heads were broken. I, however, took no part in these, excepting assuming the defensive, and threatening them with punishment if they interfered with me, being now, and having been for a long time past, quite as expert as any of them with the spear, and boomerang. After a great deal of talk and noise, all became reconciled, and there was another Corrobberree on a large scale. A little before this affair, I had taken charge of a little blind boy, and a girl, children of my supposed brother-in-law, who were very much attached to me, and went with me in my hunting and fishing excursions.

I should here observe, that the natives sometimes, and when the wind is favourable, hunt round a kind of circle, into which they force every kind of animal and reptile to be found; they then fire the boundary, and so kill them for food; it matters not what they are, whether kangaroo, wombats, opossum, or black snakes; they are to them, with the exception of the last named, all alike; as are also lizards, toads, rats, mice, and wild dogs; they cook and eat them all. On one of these burning excursions, I remember a monster snake was killed, having two distinct heads, separating about two inches from the body, black on the back, with a brownish yellow belly, and red spots all over. It had been about nine feet long, but the fire had burnt the body in two, and being such an unnatural looking monster, the natives were terribly frightened at its appearance.[3] Of the poisonous snakes generally, they are not the least afraid, for they eat them, after cutting off the heads, and roasting them in the usual manner.

With my adopted children, and two families only, I now went to a place they called Bearrock, where there was a chain of water holes, full of excellent eels, and roots, on which we subsisted for a long time. One night one of the women—just as we were laying down to sleep—heard a rustling in the bushes, as if people were approaching. Her, and her husband, came immediately, saying we must all run for our lives, and thus dreadfully alarming the little girl, and her blind brother for they had all been present at the murder of their father. After a minute's thought, we all resolved to be off, in order to conceal ourselves. Being quite at a loss what to do, we remained silent, if possible to ascertain from whence the noise proceeded, and who the strangers were. After a time, our two men, who had gone out to reconnoitre, came back, saying they had seen a fire, with several men standing round about it, which very much increased the alarm, and particularly of my poor little boy and girl. For their protection and support, I put some fire into one of our native buckets, covering it over with turf, and then moved off to a more concealed place, the natives called Banor, on the top of a small hill in the shape of a sugar-loaf, and close to the sea side, from whence, at day-light, I knew I should be able to see all around me to a great distance.

In the morning, on looking anxiously around, I observed, about a mile off, some people coming in my direction, and in consequence of their approach,

I concealed myself, with my charge. However, I soon saw they were our friends, who we had left the night before. We then held a consultation as to the direction we should take for their safety, and differing in opinion, we separated, they going one way inland, and I, with my charge, another; mine being toward a place they called Kirkedullim, near the sea side. So we kept wandering along for several days, until we made a lengthy halt at Mangowak where we lived on shell fish, and a sort of wild grape which grows in great abundance thereabout. It being the height of summer, we did not suffer much privation; for, as far as I was concerned, I had now been many years accustomed to all the habits of my extraordinary life.

Moving on again, we at length arrived at the Karaaf River, my favourite spot, where I found the hut just as I had left it months before. I know not the cause, but the natives had not visited it, or if they had, they had not in any way interfered with the arrangements I had made for my comfort. Here I again made fast my wear; and although for several days and nights we were very unsuccessful, in consequence of the tide and weather being unfavourable, ultimately a great lot of fish was taken, and we lived in abundance on bream, and roots. I had now become very anxious for the safety of my charge, particularly on account of the poor blind boy, who could in no way assist himself by getting out of danger, should any savage tribe attack us in the night, as I have already described is often their custom. I was at length relieved in part from this responsibility by the arrival of a man, with his wife and family, who I knew to be friendly to us, and who settled himself down close to our locality.

1. Weir.
2. Illness. This is evidently a typographical error in the original.
3. The identity of this red-spotted double-headed serpent remains a mystery.

CHAPTER VII

——I awoke
To hear the Ocean's never varied sound
And the wild sea-mew, wheeling round and round
Where hope, the sun light of the soul, ne'er beams
A broken-hearted Exile, e'en in dreams

Our small community remained in perfect harmony for many months, until, unfortunately, a young man about twenty years of age, belonging to another tribe, arrived. This youth was taken seriously ill a few days after joining us, and although we did all we could for him he died. This event created great distress, and by way of changing the scene, our small party broke up, and left the Karaaf on a short hunting excursion. After a time we fell in with the deceased young man's family, who, on being informed of his death, expressed great astonishment and rage, fancying it had been brought about by some unfair means on our part. This excitement arose to such a height, as to approach—what it would be mercy to describe—insanity. After a time, they forced the poor blind boy away from me, and killed him on the spot, because he had happened to be in the same hut in which the young man died, believing he had been in some way the means of his death. After this, they roasted the body in the usual manner; but whilst this was going on I left, with the little girl, moving on, and on, until meeting the tribe to which the man belonged to whom in her infancy she had been promised; I explained all the particulars of the sacrifice of her poor blind brother. They immediately vowed vengeance, and two or three of them set out for the purpose of murder, returning in a few days with the intelligence that they had killed two of the children of their enemies.

By one accession and the other our numbers had now increased to more than two hundred men, women, and children; and it may be easily supposed, that such a mob of savages could not move on long without fights and bloodshed. Seeing these things certain, I left, with the proposed husband of the little girl, and one or two families, to go back again to the Karaaf River. Having remained there some time, I resolved on surrendering my charge to her intended husband, and the wife he had had with him for many months; and positively insisted on doing so, although they were anxious that she should remain with me for some time longer. Having transferred her to the care of these people, I set off alone, determined to live by myself, in order to avoid a repetition of the scenes I had witnessed, and all farther intercourse with the natives. The direction I took was along the sea coast, but although subsisting upon shell fish principally, I now knew perfectly well how to provide myself with a change of food, and with fire to cook it, so as to make whatever it was more palatable. Although I had parted with the girl from prudential motives, I lamented very bitterly the savage death of her brother, my poor blind boy, for whom I had acquired a great affection; and who, on his part, had so many hundred times clung to me for shelter and protection.

I was now again very lonely and miserable, and whilst indulging in melancholy thoughts one day—such as cannot be described—I was most unexpectedly joined by a young native woman, who had ran away from her tribe at some distance, where it was fighting with another. She remained with me for a long time, during which I was successful in procuring abundance of food; amongst other kinds was a large sea animal, one of that sort which the natives call the Koorman, mentioned before as having visited my retreat near where I first met the natives. We found the flesh very good eating, and my female friend enjoyed the repast with great gusto: greasing herself all over with the fat, after we had made the most of the carcass, which might well be compared to bacon.[1]

My amiable young lady friend continued with me for a long time, in fact she made all sorts of excuses for not going back to her tribe, who not coming in search of her, and we not knowing of their whereabouts, were induced at length to remove for a change of hunting and fishing grounds; arriving ultimately at Danawa, where there is a considerable river, having its source in several high mountains, some way off in the interior. The scrub through which we should have had to pass, had we left the beach, being almost impassable, we were obliged to keep along the sea shore; and the weather by this time being cold and inclement, we occasionally took shelter, and slept in the caves and crevices of the rocks. This was a very suffering time, and as soon as we could, we returned again to my old fishing castle, on the Karaaf.

The reader may wonder, how it was possible for any one like myself, who had, in my earlier life, been associated with civilized beings, so to live; but I beg him to remember how many years I had led a different sort of existence, and how easy it is for the human being, as well as every other, to change his habits, taste, and I may add, feelings, when made the mere creature of circumstances. I look back now to that period of my life with inexpressible astonishment; considering it, as it were, altogether a dreaming delusion, and not reality. Perhaps there is no one living who can cast his mind back to so many years of his past life with such a multiplicity of extraordinary sensations, as have fallen to my lot to experience.

After many months we were visited by my companion's relatives, to whom she returned, and I was left once more alone, occasionally however visiting such of the friendly tribes as came to my locality. All the years I had been upon the coast, and near it, I had never seen or heard of any ship, or of shipwrecked mariners, so that

I had no hope afforded now of ever again regaining an association with civilized beings. I had seen a race of children grow up into women and men, and many of the old people die away, and by my harmless and peace-able manner amongst them, had acquired great influence in settling their disputes. Numbers of murder-ous fights I had prevented by my interference, which was received by them as well meant; so much so, that they would often allow me to go amongst them previ-ous to a battle, and take away their spears, and waddies, and boomerangs. My visits were always welcomed, and they kindly and often supplied me with a portion of the provisions they had—assuring me, in their language, of the interest they took in my welfare.

Here I may as well say, that the native language varies according to the tribe individuals belong to, each tribe having a peculiar expression of their own. The one I was with so many years, I, of course, understood perfectly, but there were others I could scarcely make out. I saw a native from the Murray River whose language was perfectly unintelligible to all of us; indeed this is reasonable, when we reflect on the difference of the dialect, or pronunciation of words, of many of the counties of England, Ireland, and Scotland. How careful then ought those persons to be, who are now known as what are called Protectors of Aborigines, when they attempt to interpret on trials in Courts of Justice. Their translations and explanations should be received with great care, in order to prevent the infliction of unjust punishments—especially in cases of life and death. Again, there is another point to be borne in mind, that is, the vindictive character of the natives, which leads them, in many instances, to give evidence founded upon revenge and falsehood. This is all very bad, but that it is true cannot be doubted.

I had almost forgotten to say, that in my wanderings about, I met with the Pallidurgbarrans, a tribe notorious for their cannibal practices; not only eating human flesh greedily after a fight, but on all occasions when it was possible. They appeared to be the nearest approach to the brute creation of any I had ever seen or heard of; and, in consequence, they were very much dreaded. Their colour was light copper, their bodies having tremendously large and protruding bellies. Huts, or artificial places for shelter, were unknown to them, it being their custom to lay about in the scrub, anyhow and anywhere. The women appeared to be most unnaturally ferocious—children being their most valued sacrifice. Their brutality at length became so harrassing, and their assaults so frequent, that it was resolved to set fire to the bush where they had sheltered themselves, and so annihilate them, one and all, by suffocation. This, in part, succeeded, for I saw no more of them in my time. The belief is, that the last of the race was turned into a stone, or rock, at a place where a figure was found resembling a man, and exceedingly well executed; probably the figure-head of some unfortunate ship.

One day when I was at Bangibarra, some distance in the interior, I saw some natives coming along, one of them carrying a flag over his shoulders. On anxious enquiry, I was told by them that they had seen a vessel laying at anchor in Port Phillip Bay, and near Indented Heads; watching her for several days, they observed her remove to another anchorage, soon after which, a boat was hoisted out and all hands left her, proceeding up the river. After watching several hours to see the coast clear, three of them swam alongside, and hoisted themselves on board, one, one way, and another, another. The first object that attracted their attention was the colours; these they soon hauled down: then they purloined rope, sails, and other things they thought would prove serviceable such as glass bottles to bark and sharpen their spears with. There were many other articles they took, but fortunately they were afraid to go down into the cabin, and so considerable property was saved from plunder. Having completed their marauding excursion, they carried what they had to land, and far back into the bush. When the crew returned and saw the mischief done during their absence, they fired off their pieces, but they were at too great a distance to do any injury to the natives. Thinking it advisable, they soon got the anchor up again, moving farther out into the bay.

This was the story they related, and great anxiety was expressed that I should lend a hand to decoy the people on shore, so as to get them into our power, with the vessel, boats, and cargo also. I did all possible to divert their attention, telling them that if they went to where the ship was, they would again be fired upon, and all killed. A few days after I saw the vessel still laying at anchor, and became almost nervously wild with desire to make myself known to those on board, so as at length to be released from captivity, and with that hope I went alone, taking with me merely my spears and other instruments for hunting and fishing. When I got to the beach abreast of the vessel, I made a large fire, thinking I should attract their attention, as several persons could be seen walking up and down the deck, occasionally looking attentively toward me, as I thought. All my efforts however were useless—the crew no doubt supposing, after the robbery on board by the natives, that the object was to entice them on shore for some murderous or mischievous purpose. I could not hail them, having lost all my English language. All that day and night I continued making signals—my heart ready to break with grief and anxiety, seeing all my efforts futile. About the middle of the next day, a boat put off from the side, coming in my direction; and, when distant only half a mile, my signals were repeated; but alas, when only three hundred yards off, the people in her hoisted sail, steering away two or three miles farther up the beach, toward a small island, where they landed. Seeing this to be a chance opening up for me, I followed as fast as I could run, and crossed over to where I supposed they were cutting wood. However, the breeze being in their favour, before I could reach the spot, they had cut as much as they wanted, put it into the boat, and shoved off, only laughing at my violent gesticulations and unintelligible cries; little thinking who I was, or that I was any other than I appeared to be in my native dress. Forgetting all this, I reproached them to myself very bitterly, thinking them worse than savages, thus to leave me in my misery. Instead of their having been guilty of inhumanity, I should have remembered the possibility and probability of their firing upon me—and particularly after the act of robbery before mentioned.

After consoling myself somewhat, I examined the spot where they had been, thinking to find—perhaps a hatchet, or some such like tool, which would prove useful. In looking about, I saw a mound of earth about the size of a grave; but I foolishly thought it might be a place of concealment for some kind of treasure; and, although money, or plate, or jewels, could not have been of the least use to me in my disconsolate condition, yet I determined to examine the mound; and began to do so, by taking off the turfs with which it was covered. Having worked some time, I was shocked at coming to the body of a white man, wrapped up in a blanket. It occurred to me to remove this covering, as the weather was very cold; and it seemed a pity to leave so good an article where it was, but I could not find it in my heart to rob the dead—even to supply my own pressing necessities; I therefore made the grave up again, covering it carefully over with boughs, and heavy stones, so to protect the body from the wild dogs.

Finding all my efforts to communicate with the ship useless, and after passing another night in great distress, I made my way back to the tribe. The vessel remained where she was for several days longer—a period to me of indescribable misery. What the ship was, or where she was bound to, or where from, I was never able to make out, in consequence of my ignorance of dates. During the period we were watching her, the natives told me another vessel had anchored nearly in the same place, a long time previous; from which vessel, two white men were brought ashore by four or five others, who tied them to trees, and shot them,—leaving their bodies bound.

A few months after these efforts of mine to communicate with the ship, I found a large boat stranded on the beach. It appeared to have belonged to a whaler, as there were eight large oars laying about her, partly buried in the sand; there were also three blankets rigged as a sail, with ropes, mast, and other articles, used by some unfortunate mariners who had been cast away. The blankets, after being washed, I spread over the boat to dry, and when that was done, a fire was visible at some distance, to which I went, and there found a party of natives cooking and eating fish, and other food. On seeing the blankets, they began capering about in their usual fantastic manner, expressing the most extravagant joy. Acting on prudential motives, and in order to preserve harmony, I cut the blankets up into several pieces, dividing them as I best could. This done, we returned to the wrecked boat, which they had evidently seen or known about before; indeed they soon told me, that a few days previous, two white men had wandered from the beach into the bush where these natives were, who received them kindly. The poor fellows were dreadfully bruised and cold—in fact, perishing from exposure, thirst, and hunger. They pointed in the direction where I had found the boat, as if trying to make the tribe understand that some accident had happened, looking at the same time very sad and disconsolate. Being well fed on fish and kangaroo, after some days they recovered their strength; the natives then tried to make them understand there was a white man—meaning myself—amongst them, and that they would go in search of me; but the poor fellows could not be made to comprehend their meaning, and went away by themselves toward the Yawang Plains.

There is no doubt but they were part of the people cast ashore in the boat. Some months after I heard that the same two men, who had been so kindly treated, were savagely murdered, whilst crossing the Yarra River, by a tribe called the Wairwaioo. I grieved very much at this melancholy event, for had I arrived in time no doubt their lives would have been preserved; and on the circumstance I reflected very seriously, expressing my heartfelt thanks to the great Creator of my being, for having brought me unharmed through so many dangers.

Several months after, when journeying alone along the beach, I found a large cask, a barrel or hogshead, partly buried in the sand, which, no doubt, had been thrown on shore from a wrecked ship. It was much too heavy for me to lift, or move in any way; so I set to work digging round about it, until I could get at the iron hoops, which I knew were valuable to the natives. At length I knocked the head in, but could not fancy what the liquid contents were, having lived so long in the bush without tasting any other drink than water. The flavour appeared to be horribly offensive, and the smell equally so. It must have been either beer or wine, not being strong enough for spirits. However, I determined on letting the whole contents go by the run, to prevent mischief—should the natives take a fancy to it— although so utterly nauseous to my palate. Having broken up the iron hoops into pieces, I some days after divided them amongst those who were most kind to me, and by these presents added greatly to the influence I had already acquired over them. Whether being so long with them was the occasion or not, but I began to fancy they were gradually becoming more docile and civilized.

The various families returned to their several camping places—except one old man, his wife, and children, who remained; and we proceeded together to a lake called Jerringot—one of a chain of that name—which supplies the Barwin River. Here the Bunyip—the extraordinary animal I have already mentioned—were often seen by the natives, who had a great dread of them, believing them to have some supernatural power over human beings, so as to occasion death, sickness, disease, and such like misfortunes. They have also a superstitious notion, that the great abundance of eels in some of the lagoons where these animals resort, are ordered for the Bunyip's provision; and they therefore seldom remain long in such neighbourhoods, after having seen the creature.

They told me a story of a woman having been killed by one of them, stating that it happened in this way. A particular family one day was surprised at the great quantity of eels they caught; for as fast as the husband could carry them back to their hut, the woman pulled them out of the lagoon. This, they said, was a cunning manoeuvre of a Bunyip, to lull her into security—so that in her husband's absence he might seize her for food. However this was, after the husband had stayed away some time, he returned, but his wife was gone, and she was never seen after. So great is the dread the natives have of these creatures, that on discovering one, they throw themselves flat on their faces, muttering some gibberish, or flee away from the borders of the lake or river, as if pursued by a wild beast.

When alone, I several times attempted to spear a Bunyip; but, had the natives seen me do so, it would have caused great displeasure. And again, if I had succeeded in killing, or even wounding one, my own life would probably have paid the forfeit—they considering the animal, as I have already said, something supernatural.

1. Fur seal or sea-lion.

CHAPTER VIII

Sleep, to the homeless, thou art home,
The friendless find in thee a friend
And well is he, where'er he roam
Who meets thee at his journey's end

One day when the old man just mentioned as having remained with us, was out with me gathering roots, we discovered two young natives coming through the marshes, and in our direction: each having a coloured cotton handkerchief fastened to the end of his spear. These they held up as high as they could, waving them about to and fro, for me to see—knowing me to be in that neighbourhood. It was evident they had met with civilized people; and, on coming up, it was explained that they had met with three white, and six black men, they had never seen before. I enquired if the strangers had any boat? and was told they had a Koorong, meaning a ship, but that she was gone, leaving the men behind;—that they had erected two white houses, which I supposed to be tents;—that they had plenty of provisions, blankets, tomahawks, and such articles;—that they had asked for some of the Kallallingurks (tomahawks), but were refused; although presents were made to the tribe near Indented Heads, of knives, and scissors, and other things.

The next piece of intelligence was very alarming,— the men saying they were in search of another tribe, to enable those they had left behind to murder the white people the more easily, and by doing so to get possession of their property.

That night was one of great anxiety to me, for I knew not how, without danger, to apprise the strangers

of their perilous situation—as the least appearance of
such an intention would, to the natives, have seemed like
treachery. My reflections were very painful, for I was, of
course, aware of having long since forgotten the language
of my youth. I was at a loss what to do for the best, but
at length determined on hazarding my life by going to
them at the earliest opportunity, for their protection. So
when the two men who brought the intelligence had left
us to go in search of the other tribe, I hastened off on my
journey to where the strangers were—which, as the
natives had described, was about fifteen miles distant; but
it must have been much more, for I did not reach it until
the next day; the weather being cold and very tempestuous. At length I arrived in sight of a long pole, or staff,
with the British colours hoisted upon it; and there I also
saw a sort of camp. I now was overwhelmed with feelings
connected with the past, the present, and the future. My
being an absconder from the operations of the sentence
imposed upon me by the authorities, and the consequences of having so done; the present, with reference to
my then unmistakable liberty, and perfect freedom from
all such consequences; and, as to the future, there was
what before me?—captivity, and probable punishment;
who could tell?

Whilst sitting in deep thought musing over all these
matters, I saw one of the white men take a bucket and

go with it to a well some way off, and when he had left it with his load, I went there also, in order to gradually recover my senses, and act upon my ultimate determination, whatever it might be.

From the well I had a good view of all about me, and observed that the natives had pitched their tents near those of the white men—the former being seated round their fires, evidently in great excitement. Presently some of the natives saw me, and turning round, pointed me out to one of the white people; and seeing they had done so, I walked away from the well, up to their place, and seated myself there, having my spears and other war and hunting implements between my legs. The white men could not make me out—my half-cast colour, and extraordinary height and figure—dressed, or rather undressed, as I was—completely confounding them as to my real character. At length one of them came up and asked me some questions which I could not understand; but when he offered me bread—calling it by its name—a cloud appeared to pass from over my brain, and I soon repeated that, and other English words after him. Somehow or other I soon made myself understood to them as not being a native-born, and so the white men took me to their tents, and clothed me, giving me biscuit, tea, and meat; and they were, indeed, all very kind in every way. My sensations that night I cannot describe, and before I closed my eyes I offered up to God fervent prayers of thankfulness for my deliverance; for although I saw great danger to the new comers, in consequence of their weakness in numbers, compared with the strength which could be brought against them, yet I thought it certain they had resources in reserve, which might be made available, even if the first party was doomed to be sacrificed.

As I have already said, I was very anxious, but at the same time grateful, believing the period had arrived for my deliverance. My sensations I cannot describe; and, as I could not explain them in my mother tongue, I showed the initials W B on one of my arms, by which they began readily to sympathize and look upon me as a long lost cast-away seaman—treating me accordingly, by giving me well cooked food, shelter, and raiment. Word by word I began to comprehend what they said, and soon understood—as if by instinct—that they intended to remain in the country;—that they had seen several of the native chiefs, with whom—as they said— they had exchanged all sorts of things for land; but that I knew could not have been, because, unlike other savage communities, or people, they have no chiefs claiming or possessing any superior right over the soil: theirs only being as the heads of families. I also knew that if any transactions had taken place, it must have been because the natives knew nothing of the value of the country, except as hunting grounds, supplying them with the means of present existence. I therefore looked upon the land dealing spoken of, as another hoax of the white man, to possess the inheritance of the uncivilized natives of the forest, whose tread on the vast Australian Continent will very soon be no more heard, and whose crimes and sorrows are fast fading away amongst other recollections of the past.

In a day or two I was quite at home with the strangers, to whom I made myself useful in any way I could, by giving them useful information about the country. They said the vessel which had landed them would be back again from Launceston in a few days; bringing—they thought—a great many people, and a further supply of provisions and working tools. By their desire, I remained at the camp with them constantly, night and day; and I did so with considerable anxiety, knowing that the tribe the two men had gone to fetch, would soon arrive, and might be disposed to follow up their murderous intentions. At length these people came in great numbers, and seeing the very few English, and small party of Sydney natives, their determination to destroy them was communicated to me, with a positive desire that I should aid them, and with a threat that I should be sacrificed with the weaker party on my refusing to do so.

I knew not how to act for the best; if I acquainted the new settlers of their great danger, they might, in the excitement, have had recourse to violence, which would have made matters in all probability worse, they being so few in number. The policy I adopted therefore, was, to seem to fall in with the views of the savages, but to induce them to delay carrying them out until the ship arrived, when I said, in support of my argument, the amount of plunder would be much increased.

This manoeuvre succeeded for a few days, but at the end of that time they became very impatient, so that I told the white men to be on their guard; and arming myself with a gun, I threatened, in strong language, the life of the first native who raised a hostile hand against the strangers; telling them afterwards, that on the arrival of the vessel they should have presents in abundance. This pacified them, and they turned their thoughts from mischief to fishing and hunting: our party, for so I must now speak, keeping a good look out every night, relieving each other at intervals, to prevent surprise. At length the vessel was made out by me whilst anxiously gazing across the bay, and I lost no time in giving the pleasing intelligence to both parties;—as for the natives, they made great rejoicings, jumping round and round me in the wildest manner, tapping me on the shoulders to show their delight at my not having deceived them;

and, of course, at the arrival of the expected presents. No doubt, their guilty consciences touched them up a little; for, remembering and referring to their murderous designs, they asked me if I thought it would be safe for them to remain, or more advisable to run away into the bush? I told them to stay where they were, as they had done no wrong, but had they done so, it would have been a very different matter; for in that case, they would, to a certainty, all have been shot or hanged.

The vessel—her name I do not recollect—kept standing up the bay until she touched upon a sand-bank, about three miles off, when Mr. Batman and Mr. Wedge, who were on board, left her in a boat; and, in order to prepare for their landing in safety, I went up to the native camp, and addressed the tribes as to the conduct they should pursue. The gentlemen I have named, on coming up to where we were—whites and blacks—appeared to be very much astonished at seeing me, and at my height, as I rose at their approach. There was a person named Gunn,[1] who had been left in charge of the party during their absence, and he soon explained who I was, and other matters. Mr. Batman asked me many questions, and I told him I arrived in a ship, the name of which I had forgotten; and, as I thought, about twenty years before—but that I could only guess, having lost all recollection of time. He then asked me if I would remain altogether with his party, and what presents it would be most advisable to give the natives? The first article I recommended was bread; so the boat was immediately sent off for two bags of biscuits, and these were distributed at a great Corrobberree we had that night; which entertainment—if it may be so called— very much delighted the visitors.

My task now was to keep alive the good understanding which existed; in that I succeeded: and in the mean time, the vessel had floated off the sand-bank, and we landed from her, provisions, blacksmiths', carpenters', and other tools.

As Mrs. Batman with her family had arrived in the vessel, they were landed also, as soon as the best accommodations that could be prepared had been made ready for their reception.

The brig sailed the following day, leaving Messrs. Batman, Wedge, and the whole party behind making permanent arrangements for a settlement.

To Mr. Wedge I had fully explained all the circumstances of my case, and my anxiety about my position, as a runaway from the *Calcutta*. That gentleman said he would represent them in the most favourable light to Lieutenant-Governor Arthur, so that I might feel safe in returning to Van Diemen's Land; for I was resolved on not doing so as a prisoner, after so many years' suffering. Mr. Wedge kindly promised to use all the interest he had to procure me a free pardon; and so I waited the next arrival of the vessel, employing myself in the meantime as an Interpreter, and as the friend of both parties, seldom leaving the camp, in case any unfortunate dispute might arise during my absence.

At length Mr. Wedge expressed a wish that I should accompany him on an exploring excursion inland; so we started with two others, and three of the Sydney blacks, reaching Keingeang (as the natives called an extensive lake) the first night; and the next day Booneewang, a rising ground of considerable height, from whence may be seen a great extent of country. Mr. Wedge here took some sketches, and I pointed out to him the falls, near a place called Woorongo, where I had caught a vast quantity of eels. Of these falls he also took a view, calling them Buckley's Falls, out of compliment to me. We passed, the next day and the following, over a great extent of fine country; now jotted with the homesteads of many an industrious and wealthy settler.

It would be useless for me to describe a country at this time so generally known; suffice it to say, Mr. Wedge was surprised and delighted with the magnificence of its pastoral and agricultural resources, making, I suppose, his reports accordingly.

I must state, however, that on this excursion we visited my old fishing hut, at the Karaaf River, and, on more than one occasion, we shot wild fowl on the rivers and lakes, in the presence of the natives; so as to occasion them to entertain great dread of the use of fire arms. I was authorised to tell those I met with, that if they would go to the settlement, presents would be made to them of blankets, knives, &c., and many promised to visit us.

For some time I found it as much as I could do to keep down their inclination for thievery, and their continual grumbling at some plan not being acted upon for seizing all they saw before them—they thinking it altogether my fault that an attack had not been made; for, although they dreaded the fire arms, they desired to surprise the party, and beat them by their numbers.

At length the vessel arrived from Hobart Town, anchoring about two miles off the land, and the boat we had left with us being launched and manned, Mr. Batman went on board.

On leaving us he told me he would make a signal by firing off his gun, if there was any good news in which I was interested. He was not long on board before he did so, and that I was delighted may be easily imagined; and I had great reason to be more so, when, on landing, he handed me a letter to Mr. Wedge, who told me all was right. The next matter of importance was, to remind him of my promise to the natives, which, as the ship had arrived, ought to be performed promptly, in order to avoid dissatisfaction. The boat was accordingly sent off again to the vessel for two more bags of biscuit, but it did not return until late, so that I was obliged to defer sharing them out that night. The next morning I did so, and Mr. Wedge showed me at the same time a free pardon from Governor Arthur, and a very flattering testi-monial of thanks for my services to the settlers. These documents were dated the twenty-fifth of August, One thousand eight hundred and thirty-five; which, strange to say, was exactly thirty-two years from the date of my landing from the ship *Calcutta*. I take this opportunity of publicly acknowledging the great kindness shewn me by Mr. Wedge, in thus procuring me my freedom, so imme-diately after my becoming known to him in such an extraordinary manner; and also my gratitude to Sir George, then Colonel Arthur, for his having so readily responded to the appeal made on my behalf. It was more than I had reason to expect from any Governor, without a previous reference to the Home Authorities; and the confidence thus placed in my future exertions to benefit the first settlers, gratified me exceedingly.

Allow me, generous reader, to throw my mind back upon the hour when I thus received deliverance from the past and present, and my long hoped for freedom for the future. Thus, in effect, I expressed myself:—'I can now, once more, raise my thoughts—my unshackled mind and hands—to Heaven, as a free man. I can now offer up my prayers of praise and thankfulness to GOD, for my extraordinary deliverance, and for His wonderful preservation of me during so long a period.—My heart beats high with joy, almost to its bursting,—and, I ask, whose heart, bounding from so many long years of solitude and captivity into freedom, could, or can, beat like mine?'

Who, after reading this brief history of my early life, and of my thirty-two years' perils and wanderings in the wilderness, whatever may be his position, will not—Hope on!—Live on!—Hope to the last.

1. Jim Gumm.

CHAPTER IX

For 'Tis a goodly sight to see
What Heaven has done for this delicious land;
What fruits of fragrance blush on every tree,
What goodly prospects o'er the hills expand

Change of the Settlement — Visit from
the Putnaroos and the Wainworras —
Mr. Gellibrand — Engage as Interpreter —
Another Arrival — First House Built —
Colonising Excitement — Disputes
between the Settlers and Natives —
Two Settlers killed.

By the same vessel which brought my pardon, there arrived also instructions from the Directors of the Company forming the settlement, for us to break up our present encampment, and take up our station on the right bank of the Yarra from its source, at a spot they had fixed upon as the site of a town; little thinking, however, it was, in so brief a space of time, to become the capital of a mighty colony, replete in itself with all that is required to found a nation of pre-eminent importance.

In consequence of these orders, every one was busily employed for two days packing up and preparing for the remove to Melbourne; then only known as a town by its marked trees, and other simple signs of such like early progress. Having put all our baggage on board, I explained to the natives where we were going to, and having so done I once more trod the deck of a ship, with feelings impossible to be explained. My sable friends were not at all pleased at our leaving, thinking we might be going away altogether; and their thoughts still being upon plunder, they did not by any means like the idea of its probable escape.

In the trip up we were unfortunate, for the wind was contrary; so we had to beat about the bay two days, but in the end reached our destination, and immediately commenced unlading the cargo—the mechanics commencing temporary workshops and dwelling-houses for the people.

Whilst thus occupied, we were visited by two of the tribes I have already mentioned, the Putnaroo and the Wainworras—the savages who murdered the two shipwrecked mariners when crossing the Yarra River. They mustered about two hundred strong, men, women, and children. I had great difficulty in keeping these people from exercising their thievish inclinations, thereby bringing on difficulties between the settlers and the blacks; and I had enough to do, so as to keep myself from the suspicion of intending wrong either to one or the other party. During all the time we were landing the cargo and storing it, sentries were mounted day and night, to prevent pilfering and disputes; but other tribes continuing to arrive, increasing their strength, it occasioned me great anxiety; because I knew, as the last arrivals had left their families behind, they came with warlike intentions, and with hopes of plunder, in case an opportunity offered. This devilry was, however, neutralized by the gentlemen in charge of the settlement making them more presents of blankets, bread, knives, scissors, and such like useful articles; with which the tribes separated, apparently satisfied with the generosity shown them, and with the promises made of further supplies on the arrival of the next ship from Van Diemen's Land.

That vessel brought several gentlemen, amongst whom was Mr. Gellibrand, and they engaged me as their Interpreter, at a salary of fifty pounds a year, with rations. Soon after this, we started on an exploring expedition, looking for land; and were out about six days, traversing in the meantime, all the country round, visiting Buckley's Falls, the Yawang Hills, and other localities already mentioned; during which journey we fell in with a man, his wife, and children, with whom I had been many months, who all lamented bitterly my having left them; but the present of a blanket happily soothed their affliction.

On our return to Melbourne, we found another vessel had arrived, bringing a cargo of potatoes and other food, and articles suited to the general wants and requirements of the settlement. A great portion of the former I daily distributed to the natives by order of the persons in charge; the bricks and building materials being appropriated to the erection of a residence for Mr. Batman, on what is now called Batman's Hill, which was the first habitation regularly formed at Port Phillip. Having been bred a bricklayer, I superintended the putting up of the chimneys, although it was so many years since I had learned the trade under my good old master, Mr. Wyatt.

Other families continued to arrive, a great excitement having been created in the adjacent colonies, by the reports made of the discovery of excellent sheep and cattle pasturage; and, particularly amongst the settlers in Van Diemen's Land, who were already induced to embark large amounts in the speculation; many others also coming amongst us for the purpose of ascertaining the value of the country thus opened up, and the propriety of changing their abodes.

All things went on very quietly, until several of the Sydney blacks, and others, began to be too familiar with the native women; and at length, one of the latter came to me, saying, she had been seized by one of the shepherds, who had tied her up, but, that when he was asleep she had broken loose, and had run away to me for protection. I considered it my duty to mention the circumstance to Mr. Gellibrand, pointing out the consequences that would ensue if this conduct was persisted in; knowing well the vindictive vengeance of the natives, who, as I have already shown, are exceedingly jealous in all such matters. That gentleman immediately sent for the man accused, but he denied all knowledge of the woman, or of the circumstances to which she had referred. Mr. Gellibrand had, however, good proof of his guilt; and therefore, after severely reprimanding him for his brutality, he dismissed him from the Company's service, and ordered his immediate return to Van Diemen's Land.

Soon after this, there arrived a Missionary, who wished to travel up the country, and being applied to, I named six natives I could trust to accompany him; and they returned with him in safety after an absence of six days. This Missionary was the late Rev. Joseph Orton.

Emigrants from Sydney and Van Diemen's Land now continued to arrive almost daily, and from the former place came several gentlemen, holding official appointments, to report on the capabilities of the country generally: Mr. Gellibrand also came again from Hobart Town. During his absence an affray had taken place between the natives and some of the settlers, in which two of the latter were killed. I know nothing of the circumstances, as the affair occurred more than twenty miles away from the settlement; excepting that the deceased were buried at Melbourne.

CHAPTER X

Heaven, from all creatures, hides the book of fate,
All but the pages prescribed, — their present state

I should here state, that a Mr. Faulkner,[1] from Launceston, had been some time settled in the colony, but he had no connection with the Company. From some cause or other, and although not knowing much of me, he represented me to be a dangerous character: as one having too great an influence over the natives. I was much hurt at his representations to my prejudice with the Company; and so, not knowing what the ultimate consequences might be, I resigned my situation; continuing however with Mr. Batman, who treated me with the greatest kindness on all occasions. I do not attribute any intentional wrong to Mr. Faulkner, believing him to have been misinformed by interested persons, and that I was sacrificed by their malignity.

With Mr. Batman I remained until the arrival of a King's ship from Sydney, having on board Captain Lonsdale, of the King's Own Regiment of Foot, my old corps, with which I had served in Holland. He came to assume the command, not only as a military officer, but as the resident magistrate of the new colony. A detachment of the Fourth accompanied him for the protection of the settlers; who were, by this time, numerous, many of them being also very wealthy, and influential. The new Commandant enquired very particularly into my history and sufferings, and ultimately offered me employ, with the same pay and advantages I had had before I was discharged from the Company's service; but considering all I had done, I said I thought myself entitled to at least an advance of pay, which was at length agreed upon; so that I was in future to receive sixty pounds per annum, and rations, instead of fifty, as heretofore. This being arranged, I began the duties of my office as Interpreter and attendant on the new Commandant, pointing out to him localities for his consideration, for the building of barracks, a store-house, and such like; Captain Lonsdale however retaining his quarters on board, until a suitable temporary building was erected for his accommodation.

After a little time, I succeeded in getting the natives to work in carrying loads of goods, building materials, and water, from place to place, where they were required; rewarding them each with boiled meat and biscuit; and this sort of employ they followed with great cheerfulness.

At the sight of the soldiers' red jackets, however, they were at first very much alarmed, associating the colour with something very dreadful.

My duty now was to visit about amongst the various settlers' families, to ascertain if the natives had been in any way troublesome, to promote a mutual confidence between the parties, and for some time I was pleased to find all things going on well; but one day, a white boy brought me word that two stock-keepers had been murdered, in consequence of their attempting to ill-use some native women when they were out gathering roots. Their screams brought some of the tribe to their assistance, and the next day, as the shepherds were proceeding to another station, having their guns and provisions fastened on a packhorse, the natives waylaid and surprised them—seizing their guns the first thing, and then murdering them. This unfortunate affair happened about seventy miles from the settlement; and this was not the only one to be regretted, for several robberies having taken place near Geelong, a native was seized, and although merely suspected, he was tied to a tree and shot; the body being thrown into the Barwin River.

I was sent, in company with two other constables, to apprehend the white man—a servant of a Mr. Fisher; and having brought him with us to Melbourne, he was fully committed and sent to Sydney for trial, there being no competent tribunal at Port Phillip.—He was acquitted, as no person could clearly prove the identity of the deceased, and other necessary particulars in cases of life and death.

Soon after this, Governor Bourke visited us, with several of the Civil and Military Officers of the New South Wales Government. As good a parade as possible was made to receive him, myself having the charge of about one hundred natives ranked up in line, soldier fashion, and saluting him by putting their hands to their foreheads as I directed.

His Excellency told me to say to them, if they were quiet and orderly they should have presents of bread, blankets, and tomahawks; all of which promises were faithfully kept within a very few hours after he had landed.

The Governor having expressed a desire to see something of the interior, I was ordered to attend him, with an escort; and crossing the Yawang Plains, we reached the Marrabul, now called the Esk River, the first night, there pitching our tents. The night following we halted near the Yallock, where we again bivouacked, remaining there several days; His Excellency, the Surveyor-General and others, taking me with them, and moving in various directions, expressing great delight at all they saw of the country in that quarter. The natives we met with in these excursions, were, through me, assured by the Governor, that if they came to the settlement, and avoided committing any offences against the white people, they should receive presents of all kinds of useful articles. These invitations and promises many of them availed themselves of, behaving very peaceably. One night whilst away from

Melbourne, the party was awoke by shocks of an earth-quake; and so heavy were they, that the sentry gave an alarm, thinking at first the natives were in upon our powder and provisions.

About this time we received intelligence that Mr. Gellibrand had again arrived from Hobart Town, in company with a Mr. Hesse, a Solicitor of that city. It appeared that shortly after landing at Geelong, they had left that place on horseback for Melbourne; but, at the end of a fortnight, great alarm was excited by the news, that they had not arrived at the latter—nor found their way back to the former. Although greatly fatigued after a very long journey, I was immediately sent on horse-back in search of them; and reaching the hut of a gentleman, nearly fifty miles distant, I remained there for Mr. Gellibrand's son, who was to meet me by appointment. No news of the lost gentlemen could be obtained by me on my journey;—and here, I should say, that they had taken with them as a guide a white man, who, according to his statement, they had discharged, in consequence of some misunderstanding about the direction of the route. On his return to his master, Captain Pollack, he stated 'That they had refused to be guided by him and that therefore he had left.' I engaged some trustworthy natives and accompanied them, hoping to trace the steps of the horses.

When Mr. Gellibrand, junior, joined me at the place appointed, we all proceeded to Captain Pollack's station, from whence, after necessary refreshment, the latter gentleman accompanied us on our search, following the course the guide said the lost travellers had taken, to the spot where they had left him. We traced the spoor of the horses, as the Cape men say, much farther on, into an extensive plain recently burnt, and here we lost it altogether. We now struck across the country, still hoping to gather some intelligence; and falling in with a native encampment, and having reason to think it was not a tribe likely to receive the white men in a friendly manner, I requested them to remain where they were, whilst I endeavoured to obtain some information. This being acceded, I approached, but being on horseback, and in an unknown dress they, at first, did not know me, but ran away in great alarm, having never seen a horse before. After a time, however, I made them understand who I was, and dismounting, they all came round me in a friendly manner. Just when I was explaining the object of my visit, our white party rode up, and one of them began asking questions in a jargon of language no one could understand; and by this interference prevented my doing any service, for I had scarcely had time to express even a hope that they would go in search and do their best to bring the lost gentlemen to the settlement.

The abrupt appearance of our people on horseback, so much alarmed the natives, that I could do nothing, except accompany them alone to their camp as they wished, but this my companions would not allow me, as their guide, to do, not feeling safe in my absence.

Our efforts to trace the lost travellers were all in vain, and at length I returned to Melbourne to report our ineffectual efforts for their rescue. Whilst we were absent on the expedition, Governor Bourke had returned to Sydney, and the news of the loss of Messrs. Gellibrand and Hesse having been forwarded to Hobart Town, three of their friends arrived with the determination, if possible, to trace their fate. I was applied to for information, and to accompany them; the former I gave them, but I refused the latter proposal, because I was certain I could do much better if I went by myself on such a mission. They appeared very much displeased at my objections, and I was summoned before the Commandant to give my reasons; to whom I said, those who were with me before had most improperly interfered, endangering my life and their own, by not having placed confidence in me and allowed me to do with, and say to the natives, what I thought best on the matter. The Commandant agreed with me, but the persons who had taken the affair in hand decided on having their own way; and they accordingly engaged several blacks to go with them, who strange to say, they furnished with fire arms.

Three days after they had left the place, I had permission from Captain Lonsdale to proceed alone on my search; but my horse having a sore back, I was obliged to remain a short time until it could bear the saddle. In the meantime he was tethered in the rear of my quarters, where the animal was very happy during his temporary rest; until one day a native came running to me in great sorrow, saying he was bleeding very much and nearly dead. Mr. Batman happening to be near, we went away together to where the horse was, and found he had been, what is called, ham-strung; all the hind sinews of his legs having been cut through by some white, or other savage.

My poor horse died, and I took passage by a vessel to Geelong, in order there to provide myself with another, and thence pursue my search, although I had long since concluded upon its being useless, after the absurd efforts which had been made by those who, no doubt, most anxiously desired to recover the lost gentlemen, but knew nothing about how successfully to accomplish so difficult an undertaking in such a country and under such circumstances. Mr. Gellibrand, junior, did all he could; and as a son, was naturally excited and influenced by all proper feelings of regret, anxiety, and perseverance; but what could he do, over-ruled as he was by others, who had done more harm than good in the search, as I have already shown, by their improper interference with me, who might have led to the discovery of the lost travellers, either dead or alive.

Having obtained permission, I at length set off alone, and at Mr. Reibey's station received intelligence that a native and his daughter had been shot by the natives who had accompanied the three gentlemen that preceded me from Melbourne by land, and who, being much alarmed at the circumstance just recorded, had returned to that place. Knowing it would be useless for me to attempt any discovery after this event, I went on board again, and returned to Melbourne also. It was an inexcusable murder, for there was not the least reason to believe that the poor people who had been so merci-lessly sacrificed, had had anything to do with the death of either Mr. Gellibrand or Mr. Hesse, neither was it known at that time whether they were dead or alive. This affair gave me great pain, because, from my long association with the natives, I thought such destruction of life anything but creditable to my countrymen; but on the contrary, that they were atrocious acts of oppression.

From that time all search after the unfortunate gentlemen ceased, but enquiries were still continued, unfortunately without effect. In Mr. Gellibrand, I lost a very good and kind friend; his humane considerations for me will never be forgotten; and amongst other evidences of this feeling, he had given me the horse which, as I have just said, was so brutally mutilated.

About this time, an absconder from Van Diemen's Land was apprehended, and ordered by the Magistrates to be returned to Launceston; and I asked permission to take charge of him to that colony, which request was acceded to, as I was a Constable. Having delivered the prisoner to the Gaoler at Launceston, I went into the country for a few days to visit an old shipmate, whose name it is not necessary to mention, and then returned for a passage back again, according to the orders I had received.

At this time a steam vessel arrived at Launceston with some prisoners bound to Port Phillip, and in her was Captain Fyans, who had been appointed Resident Magistrate at Geelong. I returned to the new colony in that vessel, having received great kindness at Launceston from Mr. Samms, the Under Sheriff, and others, who gave me flour, and other things, as presents for myself, and to be given to the natives.

On my arrival at Melbourne, I was directed to accompany Captain Fyans to Geelong, he having a number of other persons with him. On crossing the

Yawang Plains it came on to rain very heavily, and having been much occupied and exhausted before I left Melbourne, by my explanations to the friendly tribes of natives, and by my long march, I was compelled to rest by the way,—the party proceeded on without me.

I hesitated for some time whether I would follow the Captain in the morning, but at length determined to do so, and proceeded to Mr. Fisher's station, who on all occasions treated me, as had Messrs. Simpson and Wedge, with the greatest kindness and consideration; so much so, that I shall, through life, always be pleased to acknowledge the obligations I am under to them and others.

Having gone on to Geelong and remained there several days, I obtained permission to return to Melbourne by water; and, soon after my arrival, was sent in search of sheep, said to have been driven away by natives. In this way I was employed for several weeks, but finding that some persons were always throwing difficulties in the way of my interests, and not knowing what might be the result, I determined on resigning office, and on leaving a colony where my services were so little known, and so badly appreciated by the principal authorities.

It was not without great regret, that I resolved on leaving the colony, because I had believed my knowledge of the language and habits of the natives, acquired during my sojourning amongst them, might have led to my being employed by the local authorities during the rest of my life; but, when I reflected on the suspicion with which I was viewed by the most influential white men, and on the probable doubt the natives would entertain in my sincerity after having left them, I thought it best to retire to Van Diemen's Land. Indeed, I could not calculate on one hour's personal safety from either one party or the other, under such circumstances, for if lives had been lost, or cattle stolen, in any locality where I happened to be stationed, prejudice or vindictive feelings might have been brought into play, and I should have been sacrificed.

In proof of this, and of the reckless way in which conclusions were sometimes arrived at in serious matters, I will here relate, in as few words as possible, what happened to one of the natives, who, poor fellow, had a very narrow escape from death, in consequence of false information; such as I might have been subjected to at any time, had I remained in a colony where no confidence was placed in me, merely because I possessed more influence with the natives than others.

1. John Pascoe Fawkner.

CHAPTER XI

My mark of life is nearly ended;
Bugler,—sound the 'Halt!'

Charge against a Native — How sustained
— The Climate — Sail for Hobart Town —
Hospitable reception — Narrow escape from
becoming a Public Performer —
Government House — Again enter the
Public Service — My Marriage — Discharge
and Pension — Narrative draws to a close.

I have already related some of the circumstances connected with the loss of Messrs. Gellibrand and Hesse. Soon after the search for them had been given up, a vessel arrived at Geelong from Van Diemen's Land with goods and passengers; amongst them was a carpenter, who had with him a tool-chest and other baggage to carry up from the beach. By that time the natives had acquired the industrious habit of working in this way, many of them being very useful and civil, after their fashion; in fact, all those who know anything of their habits, are aware how docile those of the poor creatures are, who are well inclined, and how anxious they are to please those who employ and treat them kindly. One of this description was engaged by the carpenter to carry his traps up from the ship, and as a reward, and for the sake of decency, he was clothed in a much worn coat and trowsers; in which, having done all that was required of him, he set off to astonish his tribe by his very smart and altered appearance. He left in great glee, little thinking of what was to follow.

Some days after, another vessel arrived from Van Diemen's Land, and he, with others, went to her, looking for a job. The master of this craft seeing a native in such a dress, began to examine him after the fashion peculiar to self-constituted and many other kinds of Justices, who found their views and decisions only upon one order of thinking; namely, the infallibility of *their own* opinions—not in the least valuing those of others.

This wise sailor judge swore he knew the coat the man had on to have been the property of Mr. Hesse; that, in fact, it was the one he wore when he left Hobart Town;—that he could trace spots of blood upon it; and, on this evidence the native was seized, handcuffed, and forwarded to Melbourne on a charge of murder.

When the accused arrived there, he was brought before the Commandant, and I was required to act as Interpreter; this, however, I at first declined, having given up my connection with the Government; but considering that the life of a fellow-creature was in jeopardy, I at length consented.

A boy, in the employ of Mr. Faulkner, who was supposed to know something of the language, was interrogated as to what had passed between him and the prisoner? But I soon found the boy was altogether ignorant, and was shocked at the idea of his evidence being taken. I then questioned the accused as to how he became possessed of the clothes? He explained, by stating, that they were given him in the manner beforementioned. I asked the poor fellow if he would know the carpenter again; or where he lived, so as to enable us to obtain his evidence? He said the man had left

Geelong, and that he knew nothing about his present residence.

I explained all this to the Justices, but the Captain of the vessel persisted in the statement that the coat belonged to Mr. Hesse; so the prisoner was remanded to the guard-house. The coat was then given into my charge, with instructions that I should make every enquiry concerning its former ownership; and with that view, I gave it into the care of the Chief Constable, readily enlisting his sympathies for the native, who I believed to be innocent.

One day whilst walking along the banks of the river we were talking over the matter, particularly of the hard swearing of the Captain, and of the probable consequences to the accused: when a man, who, with his wife, was within hearing, suddenly stopped, and said he should like to see the coat; for he remembered having given a coat of the kind with other things to a native, for carrying his chests up from the Geelong beach in the manner already mentioned. We listened with great interest to his statements, and he afterwards fully proved the identity of the coat; and that the stains of supposed blood upon it were red paint marks, occasioned by himself when wearing it in his trade at Launceston. He afterwards clearly identified the prisoner as the native to whom he had given the coat and trousers; so that after an unavoidable short delay, he was discharged, greatly delighted at being liberated; although, on finding himself once more at liberty, he cried loudly and bitterly, like a child.

I make no remark upon the conduct of his accuser, who had so nearly sacrificed the life of another; but I must do the Commandant, Captain Lonsdale, the justice to say, he did all he could in the matter to administer justice free from prejudice; and that, after the case was dismissed, he ordered me to take the native to his own house, where he was received and treated with great kindness. After eating as much as he pleased, at my recommendation he was given blankets, tomahawks, and other things as presents, added to which, he received a quantity of bread and meat, to help him on his way homewards to his tribe, about fifty miles distant, over a portion of which I accompanied him, leaving the poor fellow at last in high spirits and good humour. It was a very lucky escape for him, and the circumstances are additional proofs of the danger at that time arising out of false information in any matter where the natives were concerned.

As it may be expected, that I should say something more about the localities I visited, of the climate I experienced, during so many years, and of other things and circumstances which more properly belong to the history of a country, than to that of an individual, I will add a few brief remarks.

The climate I found very genial, in temperature I suppose between that of New South Wales and Van Diemen's Land; but during the winter months, the cold winds and rains, in the country near the coast, are very trying, even to the Aborigines, who often shrink before the heavy gales into hollow trees, caves, and holes in the rocks, in a pitiable manner. In the summer months, it is not so hot as many imagine, but as the heat generates myriads of musquittoes, and of a very large sort of horse fly, the traveller suffers much inconvenience and torment. These, however, are not peculiar to Port Phillip, for in all uncleared and uncultivated countries it is the same. To avoid these insects the natives carry their lighted fire-sticks, holding them to windward.

The thunder and lightning storms are occasionally very heavy, and I have already noticed the shock of an earthquake, but I never heard of any other. There was also one heavy flood, in consequence of continuous rains, but they are not often known to exceed the supply required by vegetation.

The trees and flowers.—I have not the ability to give an account of these; neither is it necessary, scientific explorers having done so in various works, which the growing importance and natural resources of the

province have rendered it desirable to bring befo
public. The same with the birds and other creatures.
It is more especially my business, in this narrative, to
allude to the Aborigines.

The natives live to about the same age, generally,
as civilized people—some of them, to be very grey-
headed. They have an odd idea of death, for they do
not suppose that any one dies from natural causes, but
from human agencies: such as those to which I have
alluded in previous pages of this narrative. The women
seldom have more than six children, and not often so
many. So soon as they have as many as they can con-
veniently carry about and provide for, they kill the
rest immediately after birth: not to eat them—as may
be supposed—but with the idea that, for the sake of
both parties, and under such circumstances, death is
practical mercy.

To resume the thread of my narrative. I sailed from
Melbourne in the *Yarra Yarra*, on the twenty-eighth of
December, 1837, and landed at Hobart Town the tenth
of January following. On arriving, the master of the
vessel, Captain Lancey, went with me to the Bank, to
procure the value of a cheque I had, and he afterwards
took me to the Duchess of Kent Inn, where he entertained me very hospitably. In fact, on all occasions he
behaved towards me in the most generous manner.

At the Inn, I was visited by a Mr. Cutts, then the landlord of the Black Swan, Hobart Town, a country-man of mine, who insisted on my making his house my home, free of all charge; which invitation, for a few weeks, I thankfully accepted.

In my rambles about the town, I was frequently accosted by persons anxious for information about Port Phillip, with the extraordinary accounts of which all Van Diemen's Land had become, I may say, inflamed. To the new colony, vessels full of emigrants, with sheep, &c., were almost daily proceeding; so that any information from me was considered valuable. In one of my peram-bulations, I met with a gentleman who gave me a ticket to the Theatre; asking me, at the same time, to accom-pany him, which I did, and was very much gratified at what I saw. At length one of the performers came to ask me if I would like to visit the place again, and come upon the stage? Thinking his offer kind, and that I should see the performance better there, I said yes; little supposing I was to be then exhibited as the huge Anglo-Australian giant. However, the next day I found what was intended, and soon gave a denial to any such display, very much to the mortification, as I afterwards understood, of the stage manager, who had publicly notified my appearance.

About this time I was visited at Mr. Cutts', by one of my old shipmates in the *Calcutta*, who had become a wealthy and respectable settler, near the Green Ponds, about thirty miles from Hobart Town. After a few days, and he had settled his business, I accepted an invitation to accompany him to his home, where I was hospitably entertained more than three weeks; when, being tired of an indolent life, I begged my friend to make interest with his Excellency Sir John Franklin, so that I might have employ. My friend lost no time in acceding to my wishes; and, in a few days I was directed to call at Government House at an early hour, and had the honour to be introduced to Sir John and Lady Franklin, and to several gentlemen who were breakfasting there. Numerous were the questions they put to me, and amongst the rest was, what I wished on my own account? I replied, a small allotment of land! His Excellency said he could not grant land, but that he would see what could be done in the way of finding me employment.

According to this promise, I was soon afterwards appointed Assistant to the Storekeeper at the Immigrants' Home, Hobart Town; which situation I held about three months; when the immigrants having been all settled, the establishment was broken up, and I was transferred to the Female Nursery, as Gate-keeper.

At the Immigrants' Home I had become acquainted with a family—consisting of a respectable mechanic, his wife, and daughter; the former of whom, thinking to better himself, went on to Sydney; but, whilst on a journey he afterwards undertook overland to Port Phillip, he was killed by natives near the Murray River; thus leaving his family unprovided for.

The fact of his death having been ascertained, I tendered myself to the mother; she accepted me as her future husband, and we were married by the Rev. Mr. Ewing, the Episcopalian Clergyman at New Town, in the month of March, 1840.

Soon after this, I was attacked by typhus fever, and lay many days suffering very much; it being the only severe illness I had undergone in all my life. The kind attentions I received from my wife and her daughter however, under the merciful providence of God, at length restored me to health, but not to such health as I had previously enjoyed; my privations and exposure in the bush, with increased years, having, no doubt, materially damaged my naturally strong constitution.

In the year 1850, there was an alteration in the establishment at the Nursery, and I was paid off by the Convict Department, my services being no longer required, with a pension of twelve pounds per annum. With this small sum, for which I feel grateful, under all the circumstances of my case, and the industry of my wife and daughter, we contrive to live humbly and honestly; but I do entertain a hope, that something will be done for me by the local authorities of Port Phillip—now the great and wealthy colony of Victoria—when, by the means of this narrative of my life, my sufferings, services, and wants, are better, and more generally known.

My narrative is now at its close; let its details of dangers and privations serve as a moral to the young and reckless,—to all who, passing unheeded the admonitions of parents, guardians, and friends, rush heedlessly on the future, with all its trials and consequences, occasioning many bitter pangs to those who would instil into their minds motives of action, founded on religion and propriety. The want of these, or rather the abandonment of them, by me in early life, led to the sufferings I endured in after years, some of which I have here endeavoured faithfully to portray.

Finally. —To the Almighty God of my existence, I thus publicly offer up in all humility, my heartfelt prayers of thankfulness, for the great and merciful preservation and undeserved blessings he has vouchsafed unto me in all my wanderings: hoping, that when it may please Him to call me hence—I may surrender myself into his hands, with the true spirit and feelings of a Christian man.

As this page closes 'The Adventures of William

Buckley', in justice to him something ought here to be said in furtherance of his claim upon the Home and Local Governments. It is generally admitted, that had he not been at Port Phillip when the first Settlers arrived, they would, most probably, have encountered dangers and difficulties, which were averted only by his presence and influence.

It is understood, that two hundred acres of land were ordered him by Sir Richard Bourke, which grant he never received. He however yet lives, and the opportunity therefore remains to do him justice. It is not to be supposed that those who have the control of these affairs in Victoria, will rest content with his receiving the pittance of twelve pounds annually from the British Government, for services performed in Van Diemen's Land;—to think this, would be a reproach to all concerned. Let us then hope that some additional provision will be made for him, so that he may never have cause to regret (on account of poverty) his return to civilization, or the services rendered to those of his countrymen who found him in his solitude, and restored him to what he hoped would prove happiness for the few remaining years of his extraordinary existence.

In all the surrounding prosperity, arising out of the increase of flocks, and herds, and gold, surely Buckley may be permitted, in a very small degree, to participate?

His career in this island has been most respectable and praiseworthy. Under all circumstances, then, Victorians, give him a reward suited to your means, your liberal feelings, and your sense of justice.—ED.

Reminiscences of

JAMES BUCKLEY

———

who lived for Thirty Years among
the Wallawaro or
Watourong Tribes at Geelong

Port Phillip

communicated by him to

GEORGE LANGHORNE

Reminiscences of James Buckley for Thirty Years resident among the Watourong Blacks at Port Phillip taken verbatim nearly, from himself by Mr. Langhorne.

On inquiring somewhat respecting the early years of this individual, the account he gave me was somewhat confused and as follows.

I remember very little of my early years—I was born at C——ton in ——[1] where my uncle Buckley resided when I left England, but my Parents had removed sometime previous to my departure. I was apprenticed to a Bricklayer from whom I ran away and enlisted into the Regiment of foot but changed into the fourth or Kings own Regiment when that Regiment was ordered to Holland, in 1799—with the Troops under the command of the Duke of York. On my return I met with the misfortune which occasioned my being sent out a prisoner to New South Wales. One day crossing the Barrack Yard where our Regiment was quartered a woman whom I did not know requested me to carry a piece of cloth to a woman of the Garrison to be made up. I was stopped with it in my possession, the property had been stolen I was considered the thief and though innocent sentenced to transportation for life. In the year

1804 I believe,[2] I arrived here in the *Calcutta* where it was proposed to form a colony upon some part of the coast though this design was afterwards abandoned. Dissatisfied with my condition as a prisoner of the Crown and finding that the ship was about to sail for Van diemans Land I resolved to make my escape and if possible find my way overland to Port Jackson.

I made known my plan to two other prisoners and we all three succeeded in cutting away a boat and making our escape in her to the shore—where we left her to her fate and ran up the country. We pursued our way up the Port as far as the Yarra River until near where Melbourne now stands and having by this time consumed the small stock of provisions we brought with us we left a tea kettle and other articles behind us on the Bank and struck into the Bush. I wished to direct our course to the Northward in hopes by so doing to reach Sydney which I believed was not far off—here we differed and my two companions taking one direction I took the other. When however I had gone some little distance my heart failed me and in a desponding frame of mind I again directed my steps towards the sea and at length reached the Heads of the Bay in a state of considerable exhaustion. For afraid as yet to eat all the wild berries that came in my way not being acquainted with their properties and supposing some of them poisonous I subsisted principally on crawfish—suffering much from thirst. On reaching the coast I in vain looked for the Ship it had probably been gone some time.

Up to this period I had not seen any of the natives but at length I fell in with an Old Black—fishing near the sea with his wife and a large family of children. By this savage I was treated with the greatest kindness, partook of their food and laboured with them. I gradually became capable of expressing my wants in their language. I left this old man and wandered further into the Country and then fell in with several more families of Blacks. Our meeting took place thus—I was sitting under a tree near a lagoon not far from the River Barwin dispirited and almost worn out with my sad condition when some Black women made their appearance. I learnt afterwards that they had come hither to gather the gum from the mimosa³ Tree which forms a favourite article of food. I had been I believe about two months resident in the country but I do not think they had heard of me—on seeing me they retired and informed their companions who were nigh at hand—these came up and viewing me for some time with evident astonishment at length made signs to me to follow them. I immediately did so although I despaired of my life as my impression was that they intended to kill me. They took me to their encampment one black holding one of my hands and one the other. On reaching a hut or Willum near which was a Waterhole I made signs that I was thirsty and they gave me some water and without being asked offered me some gum beat up and prepared after their manner. They then all sat down and a general howling was set up around me the women crying and sobbing and tearing their faces and foreheads with their nails (a token of excessive grief)—I learnt afterwards that they believed me to be a black who had died some time since and who had come again to them in the shape of a white man.

In the evening a great dance took place, I believe in honor of my arrival—and from this time I was to them an object of the utmost care and solicitude. They never allowed me to walk any distance unattended—and if I happened to leave them for a little Blacks were immediately sent in search of me—when tears were often shed on my reappearance. I lived as they lived and was careful not to give them offence in the smallest thing—yielding to them at all times—and sharing with them whatever I took fishing or in the chase. They gave me a black woman for a wife but observing that this occasioned jealousy among others of them I relinquished her to the native and contented myself with being single—this seemed to please the men much—and I was no longer apprehensive of danger from them.

I had lived about six months with them when I fell in with one of my companions whom I found living with some Blacks on the Sea Coast. He then came and lived with me—but from his faithless conduct to the Blacks and dissolute behavior towards their women I was so apprehensive of danger to us both that I resolved to part from him—and I therefore told him that it was necessary for our mutual safety that one must leave the Tribe. He left and I never heard of him more except by a vague report that he had been killed by the Blacks—this fate I felt assured from his imprudent conduct awaited him. My other companion I never heard of after parting from him at the Yarra it is probable he met the same fate as the former and perhaps on the same account.

I now made up my mind to continue with the Tribe (Watourongs) and principally lived about the River Barwin, my favourite place of abode being the part now called Buckley falls. I soon lost all reckoning of time—I think after I had been about two years in the country I soon after was enabled to express myself in the Blacks language pretty well—so as readily to make known my wants and after a few years residence among the natives I could speak the language quite well. When I had attained this knowledge of their tongue I found I was fast losing my own—my situation however was now less irksome as I was able to converse with them respecting themselves and their connection with the different Tribes. The subject of Religion I was careful not to introduce as I was afraid that they would kill me if I meddled with their customs or superstitions. I have frequently entertained them when sitting around the camp fires with accounts of the English People Houses, Ships—great Guns etc. to which accounts they would listen with great attention and express much astonishment.

The affection of the Tribe for me always remained the same if I hinted at the probability of some day or other rejoining my own countrymen they manifested grief and shed tears. As I always kept up at night the best fire and had the best Miam Miam in the camp (the Blacks notwithstanding cold being often too lazy to attend to their fires) the children would often prefer to sleep with me and I was a great favourite among them. On one occasion feeling uncomfortable from the dirty state in which I was, it was soon after I had joined them—I repaired to the Lagoon before mentioned to wash myself. Thinking I had ran away from them as I had not mentioned my intention they were presently engaged in searching for me—an Old Man named Bow——t on discovering me among the reeds took me out by the hand and immediately burst into tears. They appeared over joyed at having found me and ever afraid lest I should again leave them.

When engaged in their fights which were very frequent when first I came among them I was always obliged to accompany them but never compelled to take a part. They would arm me with a spear and place me aside in some bush or other concealment but if discovered by the opposing party I was never disturbed or attacked. The wars between the Waworong and Watourongs have been numerous and bloody I have accompanied the latter in their night expeditions against the former when falling suddenly upon their camp they have destroyed without mercy men women and children. I have sometimes succeeded in parting them when about to fight.

I became as expert as any of them in spearing the Kangaroo and taking fish—and with regard to the latter was generally more successful when fishing alone. My practise was to light a fire as a signal to the Blacks in the neighbourhood to come and partake of my spoils which they never failed to do. Besides the Kangaroo, O'possum, Bandicoot and Sugar Squirrel[4] they seek with great eagerness for the Hedgehog or porcupine[5] which forms a delicious article of food—in order to obtain it from its hiding place they put into the hole a young child with its legs foremost who feels how and where the animal is situated and reports accordingly in what part he is to be obtained by digging into the earth as the holes run under and parrellel with the surface for some distance. Their method of dressing it when obtained is this. They enclose it entire in a piece of Bark and thus roast it—then taking off the skin again apply the body to the fire. Thus dressed it is considered a great treat.

I have noticed at least four different Tribes who speak as many different dialects—the family or portion of a tribe with whom I spent the greatest part of my time was called the Wattewarre—in their wars I observed one circumstance worthy of notice—should they happen to lose their spears, they make afterwards but faint efforts and appear to give all up for lost. It is true they are cannibals—I have seen them eat small portions of the flesh of their adversaries slain in Battle —they appeared to do this not from any particular partiality for human flesh but from the impression that by eating their enemies they would themselves become more able warriors. Many of them are disgusted with this ceremony and refusing to eat, merely rub their bodies with a small portion of fat as a charm equally efficient. They eat also of the flesh of their own children to whom they have been much attached should they die a natural death—when a child dies they place the body in an upright position in a hollow tree and allow it to remain there until perfectly dry when they will carry it about with them.

On the subject of Religion as I said before I never conversed with them I do not believe that they possess any distinct notion of a Supreme Being or of the Soul or Spirit. I have heard them warn their children not to frequent the neighbourhood of a grave otherwise I have not observed that they have any superstitious dread of particular places. There are however two imaginary Beings whom they treat with a certain degree of respect. One of these is supposed to reside in a certain marsh and to be the author of all the songs which he makes known to them through his sons. The other is supposed to have charge of the Pole or Piller by which the sky is propped—Just before the Europeans came to Port Phillip this personage was the subject of general conversation it was reported among them that he had sent a message to the Tribes to send a certain number of Tomahawks to enable him to prepare a new prop for the sky as the other had become rotten and their destruction was inevitable should the sky fall on them. To prevent this and to supply as great a number of Iron Tomahawks as possible—some of the Blacks repaired to Western Port and stole the Iron work from the wheels of the Sealers cart.

It is about 25 years since I first saw an European Tomahawk among them—on enquiring where they

obtained it they informed me that while I was a[
some distance in the interior some white men had
rowed up the Barwin in a Boat and had left the
Tomahawk at the place where they landed. On visiting
the spot I observed the place where the strangers had
dug to procure water. The Natives Tomahawks
(merang) are made of talc[6] shaped in an oval form and
placed in a bent stick the two ends of which are firmly
bound together.

A syphylis disorder is very prevalent among them—
attacking not only the adults but the children.
Promiscuous intercourse of the sexes is not uncommon
and in certain festivals is enjoined—at certain times the
women are lent to the young men who have not wives.
The women in other respects are faithful to their
husbands. Sometimes a Black will go to a Willam or
miam miam to entice a woman away should the
husband be within he will give permission to her to
follow him and on her return will probably snatch a fire
brand from the fire and beat her severely.

During 30 years residence among the natives I had
become so reconciled to my singular lot—that although
opportunities offered, and I sometimes thought of going
to the Europeans I had heard were at Western Port I
never could make up my mind to leave the party to whom
I had become attached. When therefore I heard of the

arrival of Mr. Batman and his party it was some time before I would go down as I never supposed I should be comfortable among my own countrymen again.

1. Langhorne's handwriting is indecipherable here.
2. In fact 1803.
3. Wattle.
4. Sugar glider.
5. This account confuses the echidna and the wombat.
6. Diorite.